Discove
the Truf

IN HISTORY, IN ITS HABITAT, IN THE KITCHEN

Slow Food Editore

Discovering the Truffle
is a Slow Food manual

Italian edition
Alla scoperta del tartufo
Slow Food® Editore © 2013

Texts by
Grazia Novellini

In collaboration with
Ente Fiera Internazionale del Tartufo Bianco d'Alba/International Alba White Truffle Fair Organizing Committee
Centro Nazionale Studi Tartufo/National Truffle Study Centre
Organizzazione Internazionale Assaggiatori Tartufo/International Organization of Truffle Tasters

Editing
Isabella Gianicolo, Bianca Minerdo, Letizia Palesi

Translation
Carla Ranicki

Graphic design and cover
Undesign

Layout
Roberto Fidale

Photographs
Davide Dutto/Ente Turismo Alba Bra Langhe Roero Archive
City of Alba Photo Archive
Marcello Marengo/Slow Food Archive
Stefania Spadoni/International Alba White Truffle Fair Organizing Committee
Tino Gerbaldo, Bruno Murialdo

Illustrations
Massimo Ricci

Printed in October 2014
by Grafica Veneta S.p.a, Trebaseleghe (Pd)

Slow Food® Editore © 2014
All rights reserved by copyright law

Slow Food Editore srl
Via della Mendicità Istruita, 45 – 12042 Bra (Cn) – Italy
Tel. +39 0172 419611 – Fax +39 0172 411218
editorinfo@slowfood.it
www.slowfood.it / www.slowfood.com

Publishing director
Marco Bolasco

Editorial coordination
Chiara Cauda

ISBN 978-88-8499-368-7

Contents

The Truffle Zone in a UNESCO Landscape

This book about truffles, straightforward and packed with information, is based on the experience and knowledge of the National Truffle Study Centre, the International Organization of Truffle Tasters and the oldest and largest Truffle Fair, all based in Alba, and Slow Food, the international movement started in the 1980s between the Langhe and Roero. Currently dozens of towns in Italy, many united in the Association of Truffle Towns, are committed to raising the profile of the prized and uncultivable Italian white truffle, known as *Tuber magnatum* Pico, the Acqualagna white truffle or the Alba white truffle.

In Piedmont white truffles have been found for centuries on the tables of the Savoy royal dynasty and other noble families, but they were also eaten by the countrypeople who sought them out with their dogs. In the 20th century, Giacomo Morra (1889-1963), a restaurateur in Alba, played a huge role in elevating the status of this precious underground fungus, first proposing a special fair, then developing truffle promotion at a national and international level. His actions were not only beneficial for the Langhe, Roero and Monferrato but also boosted other truffle regions.

Since then, the area around Alba has developed into a real white truffle "zone", a depository of knowledge and professional skills, where the appeal and widespread use of this highly fragrant fruit of the earth has grown along with international tourism and the prestige of the area's great wines and cuisine. Tourists from all over the world are increasingly travelling to the hills of southern Piedmont, covered with woods, hazelnut groves and grapevines and dotted with small villages and castles. These hills are home to the vineyard landscapes recently included by UNESCO on its list of World Heritage sites.

Antonio Degiacomi
President of the International Alba White Truffle Fair

White Truffles? Let's Eat Them Here

"Barolo is democratic, or at least can become so" was one of the slogans of the Free and Praiseworthy Association of the Friends of Barolo with which we rascals in early 1980s Bra sneered at the pompous confraternities of gourmets. (Unexpectedly, even to us, our somewhat studenty parody developed first into Arcigola and then Slow Food.)

Could we then, or now, apply that motto to the truffle? To the most prized of the black truffles, yes: *Tuber melanosporum* can be cultivated, and multiplying the number of mycorrhized trees would have none of the adverse effects caused by an increase in the surface area planted with nebbiolo vines. But *Tuber magnatum*, the Alba white, for us Piedmontese "the" truffle, no: it cannot be cultivated, it grows only in specific environments in a limited number of places, it ripens for a brief period of the year, it is hard to locate and collect and there are ever fewer of them. And so there are not enough for everyone, or rather: there are not enough for everyone at the same time. But if all the people around the world for whom food is as much a source of emotions as a physiological need decided to plan a trip to the Langhe at some point in their life, or to one of Italy's handful of other truffle areas, then many of us could, at different times, share in the pleasure and the pride of having tasted a real miracle of nature.

So, to my friends working to promote the Alba white truffle, I say: let us explain to potential consumers what it is (as this book strives to do) and stop coming up with new systems for preserving it so that it can exported around the world. Lovers of good food can come here to eat what little there is, fresh, fragrant and perfumed. Let us stop, above all, palming off to a naive public that plethora of "truffle-flavoured" products engineered from synthetic chemicals. Democracy is first and foremost transparency and honesty.

Carlo Petrini
International President of Slow Food

Chapter I

Characteristics and Varieties

A Very Special Fungus

> More than to a fungus, more than to a rare food, the truffle should be compared to a work of art.
>
> Jean-Paul Aron
> *Le Mangeur du XIXe siècle*
> Laffont, Paris 1973

What Is a Truffle?

Botanically speaking, truffles are fungi belonging to the *Tuber* genus (Ascomycota division, Pezizales order, Tuberaceae family).

Mutualistic fungi (symbionts) live off of other species but repay the hospitality by providing them with useful substances, for example receiving sugars and giving back mineral salts. When the symbiosis between a fungus and a plant is located on the plant's root system, this association is known as mycorrhiza.

The species in the *Tuber* genus are fungi that complete their entire life cycle underground (hypogeous), in symbiotic association with trees. Truffle is the common name used for the fruiting body of the various species. Originating from the mycelium, the vegetative part of the fungus, formed of filamentous cells called hyphae, the fruit is a generally spherical mass formed by an external layer (the peel or peridium), either smooth or – more frequently – wrinkly and furrowed, and by an internal mass (the flesh or gleba) run through by veins that surround sac-like structures (asci) containing the spores (reproductive cells).

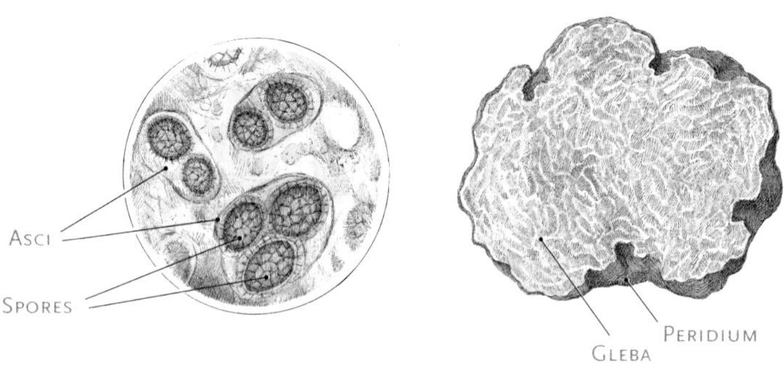

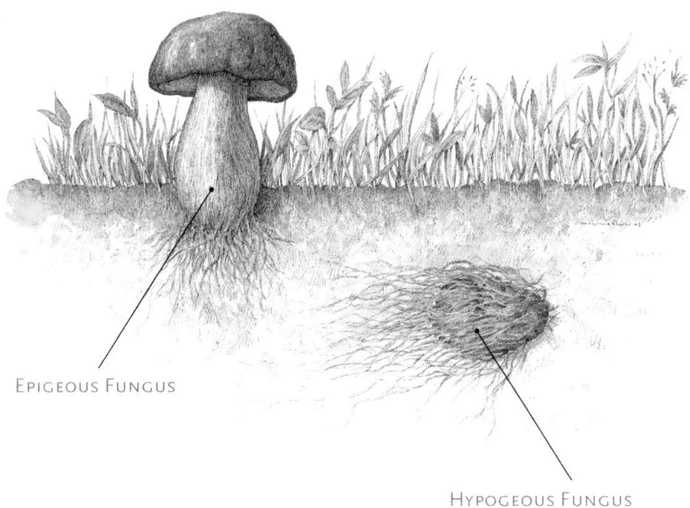

The Main Species

Around 60 species of fungi in the world are currently classified as *Tuber*, of which 25 are found in Italy. Only nine, however, are considered edible, six of which are most commonly found on the market:

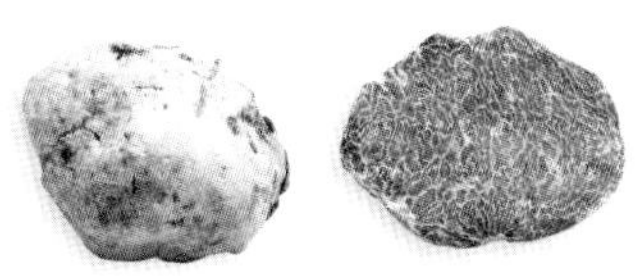

• TUBER MAGNATUM PICO
(white truffle or Piedmont, Alba or Acqualagna white truffle)

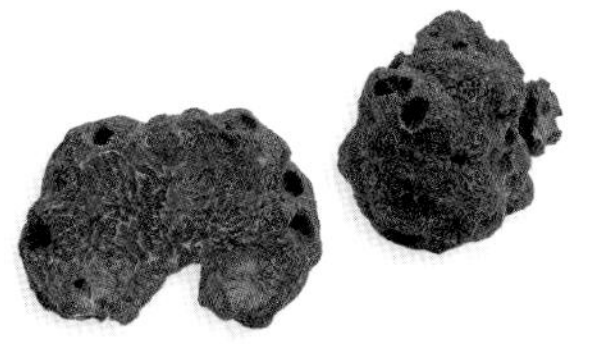

• TUBER MELANOSPORUM VITT[ADINI] OR T. NIGRUM BULL.
(black truffle or Norcia or Spoleto black truffle)

• TUBER AESTIVUM VITT.
(summer or scorzone truffle)

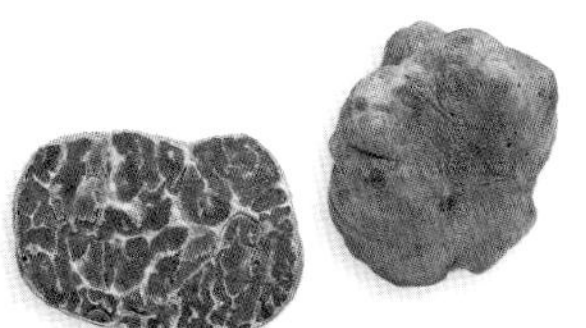

• TUBER ALBIDUM PICO OR TUBER BORCHII VITT.
(bianchetto or marzuolo truffle)

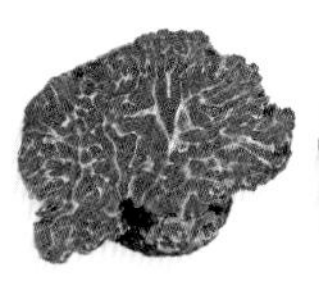

• TUBER BRUMALE VITT.
(black winter truffle)

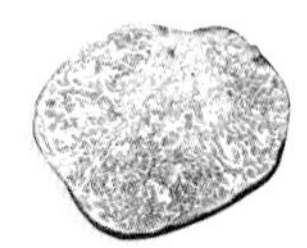

• TUBER MACROSPORUM VITT.
(smooth black truffle)

These truffles, plus another three species or varieties (*Tuber brumale* var. *moschatum* Ferry – moscato truffle; *Tuber uncinatum* Chatin – uncinato or Fragno black truffle; *Tuber mesentericum* Vitt. – common black or Bagnoli black truffle) are allowed to be hunted, collected and sold in Italy.

The Most Prized

The Alba or Acqualagna white truffle is spherical in shape, often flattened and irregular, with lobes, cavities and protrusions. The peridium is smooth, at most slightly papillate, and pale yellow or tending towards greenish or ochre, sometimes with reddish-brown blotches. The gleba, crossed by many thin, sinuous, branching white veins, varies in colour from milk white to pink to hazelnut to brown. Truffles can grow to the size of a large apple, and exceptionally examples can be found weighing over a kilo. Truffle hunting is allowed from late summer to early winter, but the white truffle reaches full maturity around the middle of October. This fungus only grows wild, and to date no cultivation techniques exist. As well as certain Italian regions, it is also found in Croatia (where production has been concentrated in Istria since the 1930s), Romania and Bulgaria.

Tuber magnatum Pico is mainly found in three areas of Italy: the Piedmontese hills, the Po Valley and the central and parts of the southern Apennines.

Piedmont's truffles, particularly those found in the area of the Langhe, Roero and Monferrato and extending into the hills east of Turin, have an undisputedly high reputation. This is the Italian region with the most extensive truffle-producing territory and therefore where the largest number of white truffles are found.

Tuber magnatum is also found in Lombardy, Emilia-Romagna, Tuscany, Umbria, the Marche (where Acqualagna, a town of around 4,500 inhabitants along the Roman consular road, Via Flaminia, has given its name to one of the white truffle's denominations), Lazio, Abruzzo, Molise and Basilicata.

The Norcia or Spoleto black truffle is round, at times with lobes, with a warty brownish-black peridium. The gleba is ebony black or purplish brown in colour, crossed by thin, pale, branching veins. It can be as big, or bigger, than a large apple. The truffles are found from mid November to mid March, particularly in January and February. The black truffle is common in much of Italy and many other European countries, from Portugal to Bulgaria, but especially in France (famed as the *truffe noire du Périgord*) and Spain. This truffle has been cultivated since the 19th century, first in France and then in the rest of Europe, with excellent results.

In Italy, it is mostly found in the central Apennines, particularly in Umbria and the Marche, but *Tuber melanosporum* can also be found between Piedmont and Liguria and in Lombardy, Lazio, Abruzzo and Campania.

Other Species

The scorzone truffle (*Tuber aestivum*) has a distinctly warty peridium, rough to the touch, black or brownish, and a gleba varying in colour from dull yellow to hazelnut, marbled by numerous whitish veins. Less demanding than other truffles in terms of climate and soil composition, it grows in association with broadleaf trees in various types of terrain, in an area that stretches across Europe and into some parts of North Africa and Turkey. It matures between May and the end of summer.

Spherical, without orifices or cavities, with a diameter only rarely exceeding 5 centimetres, the bianchetto or marzuolo (*Tuber borchii* or *T. albidum*) has a thin, smooth, frosted peridium, dirty white, pale yellow-brown or reddish yellow in colour, and a purplish- or reddish-brown gleba, run through by whitish or reddish-white veins. It grows in association with broadleaf trees and sometimes conifers, in soil that is loose and sandy, but also chalky-clayey. Its adaptability to different soil and climate conditions makes it a ubiquitous species, found in much of Europe; in Italy it is collected between February and March.

As suggested by its name, the winter truffle (*Tuber brumale*) matures with the cold. Its spherical body has a slightly warty peridium, black or bluish black in colour. The gleba is brownish grey or smoke grey, with white veins. It prefers deep soil, including clay, and tolerates standing water and the higher acidity that characterizes, for example, conifer forests.

The smooth black truffle (*Tuber macrosporum*) fruits between September and December. Often several are found in the same hole, ranging in diameter from 1 to 6 centimetres. Spherical, it has a reddish-brown or blackish peridium, with many flattened polygonal warts very close to each other, giving it a smooth appearance. The gleba, first whitish brown, then rusty brown, has many white veins, which turn pale brown on contact with the air. It likes the same habitat as the white truffle, but is more tolerant of drought.

The moscato truffle (*Tuber brumale* var. *moschatum*), a variety of the winter truffle with the same

symbiont plants and distribution range, is medium-small in size and has an irregular shape. The peridium is dark, at times reddish, with small warts that tend to fall off when handled. The grey or brown gleba has wide white veins. It matures in February and March.

The uncinato truffle (*Tuber uncinatum*), known in France as the *truffe de Bourgogne* or *de Champagne*, is collected in the autumn. It belongs to the same species as the scorzone, but is distinguished by the hooks on its spores, visible with a microscope.

This brief list of underground fungi concludes with the common black truffle (*Tuber mesentericum*), similar in appearance to *melanosporum*, though generally smaller and sometimes kidney-shaped. The black or brownish peridium has flattened warts. The gleba varies in colour from dull yellow to grey-blue and is streaked with a maze of pale veins. It ripens from September until the first months of winter, and sometimes until the spring.

The Environment and Truffle-Producing Trees

Specific environmental, weather and soil conditions are necessary for *Tuber magnatum* to develop. The soil should ideally be marly-chalky, marly-clayey or marly-sandy, characteristics shared by the geological horizon formed during the Tertiary period – the Langhian, Serravallian, Tortonian and Astian ages, for example. The terrain should have an altitude of less than 700 metres above sea level, with a moderate slope, aerated but not excessively permeable soil, moisture in the surface layers even in the driest months, a fair amount of limestone, low phosphorous and nitrogen, high potassium and a neutral or subalkaline pH. It should receive spring and summer rains and be close to waterways but with no stagnant water.
This type of environment is favourable for the following symbiont trees: English oak (*Quercus robur*), Turkey oak (*Q. cerris*), sessile oak (*Q. petraea*), downy oak (*Q. pubescens*), black poplar (*Populus nigra*), silver poplar (*P. alba*), Carolina poplar (*P. deltoides carolinensis*), aspen (*P. tremula*), goat willow (*Salix caprea*), white willow (*S. alba*), linden (*Tilia platyphyllos*), hop hornbeam (*Ostrya carpinifolia*) and hazel (*Corylus avellana*).

Tuber melanosporum requires chalky, stony soil, with a compact subsoil, rich in calcium carbonate and low in phosphorous and nitrogen. Geologically speaking, this type of terrain was produced by the breakdown of rocks during the Mesozoic era. Because the fungus needs warm soil, heated by direct sunlight, the tree cover must be no more than 30%.

Symbiont plants for the Norcia black truffle are downy oak (*Quercus pubescens*), holm oak (*Q. ilex*), Turkey oak (*Q. cerris*), linden (*Tilia platyphyllos*), hazel (*Corylus avellana*), hop hornbeam (*Ostrya carpinifolia*) and rockrose (*Cistus incanus, albidus, crispus, salvifolius*, etc.).

Sessile oak

English oak

Downy oak

Black poplar

Silver poplar

Carolina poplar

Aspen

Goat willow

Holm oak

Rockrose

Hazel

Truffle Towns

Based on the example of the Italian National Association of Wine Towns, and following similar initiatives for olive oil, bread and hazelnuts, the Associazione Nazionale Città del Tartufo (National Association of Truffle Towns) was founded in Alba in October 1990 with the aim of promoting this precious fungus, spreading the truffle culture, protecting truffle quality, encouraging the safeguarding of environmental values, strengthening truffle-related businesses and developing sustainable tourism in truffle-producing areas.

Founded by seven municipalities and three mountain communities, the association currently unites over 50 municipal administrations.

White and black truffle distribution in Italy

Chapter 2

Truffle Hunting Past and Present

Man and Dog
The Perfect Partnership

Unlike those fungi that develop their fruiting bodies above ground, hypogeous fungi cannot take advantage of air currents to spread their spores. Evolution has therefore given them a strong odour, perceptible only when mature. This attracts insects, molluscs, reptiles and mammals who feed on the truffle and spread its spores.

If they are not fortunate enough to come across a "grey diamond" so large or buried so shallowly that it breaks the surface of the soil, plenty of animals are willing to go to the trouble of digging in order to devour a truffle. Mammals who do this include the by-now very rare brown bears and wolves, as well as foxes, wild boars, pine martens, badgers, dormice, mice and rabbits. Truffle-eating reptiles include snakes and lizards; insects include grasshoppers, cicadas, crickets, praying mantises, flies, beetles, silkworms and cochineal insects; molluscs include snails and worms include nematodes. They can all potentially cause damage to the fruiting bodies and to the roots of the symbiont plant, but their greed can help the species reproduce by spreading the spores, which are transported from one place to another on the animals' paws or other body parts. Alternatively, the spores might remain in the earth with the fragments of truffle crushed by the animal's messy search.

Hunting Truffles

Without the help of a "digging" animal it is almost impossible for humans to find truffles, particularly *Tuber magnatum*, which can be buried at a consider-

able depth (up to one metre). For this reason, domestic or domesticated animals with a particularly good sense of smell have long been trained to find the fungus without swallowing or biting it, delivering it instead to their owner. First pigs and then dogs were used for centuries in Western Europe; canines are preferable because they are faster, more docile and more obedient.

The human-dog pairing is an essential part of the economy, history and poetry of the truffle. Professional hunters – who carry out the activity in order to make a profit, even if it is not their only job – are mysterious characters, almost mythical, and an integral part of local colour. The prototype of this fascinating human category is undoubtedly the Piedmontese *trifolao*, the only Italian truffle hunter to boast a specific dialect name (pronounced and sometimes seen written *trifulau*, with the variations *trifolau* and *trifulé*) as well as a well-established mythology. Descriptions of the figure, even in recent texts, tend to be somewhat stereotyped, sticking faithfully to clichés that probably had little validity beyond the 1970s. Encapsulating the truffle hunter's current identity is not simple, given the diversity within the large group of Piedmontese *trifolao* (more than 4,000 are licensed to hunt truffles). But we will give it a try, with the help of research carried out by the University of Turin's Department of Agricultural, Forestry and Environmental Economics and Engineering for the Piedmont Regional Authority's Mountain and Forest Economics Office.

A Trifolao's Talents, Motivation...

The main characteristics of a trifolao are an unparalleled knowledge of the local area, sharp powers of observation and an instinct for recognizing the best truffle-hunting places, a remarkable accord with their dog and great skill in extracting the truffle ("it takes the precision of a surgeon and the delicacy of an archaeologist" says an expert) so as to keep it intact and safeguard the spores.
At the start of the 20th century, the trifolao was mostly aiming to supplement the meagre income provided by farming. The products of the forest (firewood, game, chestnuts, berries and, in the Langhe and Monferrato, truffles) represented a val-

uable contribution to the domestic economy. Truffles were collected mostly at night, to better avoid the competition and because the days were spent working in the fields. These days, truffle gathering is still a supplementary activity, but is no longer essential to the hunter's survival.

Dozens of Piedmontese trifolao were interviewed for the University of Turin study. The results show that around half of those questioned hunt or cultivate truffles professionally, while the others are primarily dealers, and one is purely a hobbyist, because everything he finds, he uses himself. During the period allowed by the regional calendar, they all visit the truffle woodlands daily – both in the daytime and at night – in line with what their regular working hours allow. In general they each use only one dog, or occasionally two. They hunt on their own land or go to historically fruitful locations, which each trifolao keeps secret. The majority hunt white truffles, but given their scarcity, it is becoming more common to collect the black summer truffle as well, as there is a market for it too. They sell mostly to dealers and restaurateurs, followed by private clients, while markets are rarely attended.

When it comes to the main problems they face, the interviewees highlighted the anthropogenic pressure caused by illegal, amateur or greedy hunters; a lack of enforcement of regulations; and environmental degradation (reduction in production capacity, lack of adequate incentives to maintain symbiont trees, reduced maintenance of the land, overly deep agricultural operations, the cutting down of many trees).

... and Assistant

Dogs are essential to the hunt. They must have good physical stamina and a highly developed sense of smell and be obedient to their masters. Over time, humans have carefully selected hunting breeds and used them for finding truffles. Among the most suitable are the Spinone, the Brittany, the Bracco, the Pointer and the Lagotto. However, it is unlikely that the trifolao's companion will be a pedigree: generally, medium-small mongrels are preferred, known affectionately in Piedmont as *taboj* (pronounced *tabui*).

Crossbreeds are popularly believed – not without reason – to have a better nose, greater stamina and more intelligence than pedigree dogs. This preference for mongrels was confirmed by the University of Turin study. In almost every case, those interviewed had crossbred dogs (though they preferred to take one at a time on a hunt, they usually owned several), with one parent a Brittany or a Bracco. The unanimous opinion is that bitches are more docile and easier to train. The price of a five-year-old dog can reach as high as 8,000 or even 10,000 euros. But trifolao, particularly professionals, prefer to train their dogs themselves. The new pup will be taken around with an older dog and will practice sniffing out truffle crumbs or wads of cotton wool soaked in truffle-infused

oil. The training begins early, when the dog is still young, and the exercises are presented as games. Candidates for the role of trifolao assistant in the Alba area can also attend a special university (see page 38).

Equipment

A truffle hunter's kit is simple and minimal: a stick with a curved handle for support on the steepest slopes and to move away soil and leaves from the base of tree trunks, a torch for lighting up the place where the dog starts digging, a tool (a small hoe in northern Italy, a small spade in the central-south) for completing the excavation and carefully and delicately extracting the truffle; a basket or knapsack for carrying the finds; some kind of consolation for the four-legged member of the team, who must be rewarded for sniffing out the right scent and then immediately standing back. During the peak season of autumn, a standard outfit would include wool trousers or heavy jeans, hiking shoes, a multi-pocketed hunter's jacket and sometimes a scarf or hat for protection against the fog and damp. Other traditional attire, like a *folar* (neckerchief), a short cape and a felt brigand's hat, belongs to a stereotype of the past. These days, some trifolao don't venture into the woods without a sat-nav...

⁂ The Trifolao of the Past

"The truffle hunter, in dialect 'trifolau', has a fairly complex personality [...]. He trains his dog, or buys it already trained. He works alone, so as not to share the treasures he finds or reveal where he goes. It is unlikely that he will show his colleagues the fruits of his searches, so as not to arouse too much curiosity and tempt them to search the same areas. He is sly, to the point of hiding small, insignificant pieces of truffle in the most unexpected and difficult places, so that other truffle hunters spend hours occupied on a fruitless quest, deceived in good faith by their dogs. He is envious and might even stretch to poisoning a rival's dog. He is dignified in all his outward displays; his is a contained joy, never explosive and contagious.

He has a personal calendar, an instinctive topographic map that every year leads him to search the wooded valley floor with exactitude, and on Saturdays he sets off for Alba, where it takes only a few minutes to relish the pleasure of a sale.

There is no 'breed' of truffle dog. In practice the truffle hunter prefers a dog of modest size, who will be easier to control.

We must remember that in the majority of cases the hunt takes place at night, in the dark, and this means the trifolao must be able to count on a collaborator who is not overly lively, and will not, out of exuberance, run out of the radius of light cast by a regular portable lantern. The coat should, if possible, be pale, in order to be able to easily spot the dog in the darkness. The dog is trained for the hunt by using a refined technique by which the animal becomes exhilarated by the scent of the truffle. With rags soaked in camphor, then pieces of truffle given to the dog as food, its sense of smell is stimulated. Their sensitivity means they can detect the odour of a truffle underground, even at a distance of 15 or 20 metres.

For every truffle found, the hunter will give the dog a piece of bread as a reward, in order to maintain the conditioned reflex by which every hunt corresponds to a mouthful of food [...]."

Once the dog has followed its nose and started to scratch the earth, the hunter moves the animal away and with great care begins to dig with a special little hoe until he finds the precious truffle. Every hunter knows the places where truffles can develop, and so he heads towards poplars, willows, oaks and lindens. As, like all fungi, truffles reproduce by spores, once the "mother" plant has been discovered one can be certain that truffles will always be found in that same place and usually around the same time of year. This is the reason for the aura of secrecy that surrounds the hunt, in an attempt to ensure no one else discover these places. Because of this, and also because they normally spend the day working in the fields or vineyards, the truffle hunters work at night, in the dark, illuminating the tricky paths with pocket torches.

The market is also governed by its own rituals. Truffles are shown with circumspection and only after direct personal contact with the potential buyer.

Unlike all other markets, where merchandise is gaudily displayed to the public, the truffles remained wrapped in paper or rough cloths, stored in pockets

or baskets, while furtive glances judge the buyers and evaluate intentions and possibilities."

Renato Ratti, *Il tartufo bianco d'Alba*, Quaderni del Museo Ratti dei Vini di Alba, Abbazia dell'Annunziata, La Morra s.d. [ma 1973]

Canine Champions

An overall, historic ranking of champion truffle dogs has seemingly never been compiled, though at the first Truffle Fairs it was common to award prizes to the most prolific hunters in pairs, with bipeds and quadrupeds together on the same podium. Oral tradition and the records of the University of Roddi do however give the particulars of a few outstanding champions with simple, homely names, suited to pups of humble lineage: Dora, Zara, Bill, Leo, Pomìn, Frick. Pulìn, it seems, was a super-champion in the 1970s, who had a home-team advantage as the *tabui* of Pasquale Monchiero, one of the two Baròt IIIs (see below): a cross between a Spinone and a bitch of undefined breed, it is said that in one night he found a grand total of five kilos of truffles.

✻ A School for Tabui

Roddi, a village just outside Alba, curls snail-like around its now state-owned castle, which in the past has belonged to the Pico della Mirandolas, the Della Chiesas of Saluzzo and Carlo Alberto of the House of Savoy. *Baròt* is the Piedmontese dialect name for the wooden stick used by truffle hunters and, in Roddi, also the name of the branch of the Monchiero family that has run the University of Truffle-Hunting Dogs for four generations. This unique institution was started informally in 1880 but made official in 1935 by Count Gastone of Mirafiori, nephew of Vittorio Emanuele II and La Bela Rosin and president of the Alba Truffle Fair from 1930 to 1940.

The current holder of the title of Magnificent Rector is Giovanni Monchiero, known around the world (literally, given that like his predecessors he has been interviewed by journalists from all over the planet) as Baròt IV. A trifolao, naturally, out of passion and a family tradition dating back at least to his great-grandfather Antonio, Baròt I, the founder of the academic dynasty whose intervening members have been Giovanni's grandfather Giovanni Battista (Baròt II) and his father Pasquale and uncle Pietro (who reigned simultaneously as Baròt III).

The head of the family, Antonio Monchiero was a wise and enterprising farmer. As was common in all rural areas, then as now, he interspersed work in the fields with hunting, fishing and gathering wild foods, particularly mushrooms and truffles. Antonio sold the most valuable fruits of these endeavours to the chefs at the castle of Pollenzo, a Savoy royal residence which was rarely visited by Carlo Alberto's successors, Vittorio Emanuele II and Umberto I. The castle only returned to favour during the time of Vittorio Emanuele III, who kept his coin collection there and wanted to take the title of Count of Pollenzo when he abdicated the throne in 1946. Nevertheless, the first Baròt was still a supplier to the royal house. Aware of the talent needed to properly train a *can da trifole*, a truffle-hunting dog, it was he who had the idea of starting a university. Today, a small truffle museum is attached to the school, which still graduates the best four-legged finders of "grey diamonds" following an intensive course of two or three weeks and the pay-

ment of a modest boarding fee. Lessons are held outdoors, first in the university's courtyard, where the students learn to recognize the truffle scent by playing with balls of rags soaked in strong-smelling substances (the cruel methods of the past, when the pups were kept starving for days, are no longer allowed). They are then taken to the wooded, rocky countryside around the Tanaro River to put into practice what they have learned, initially with fragments of *Tuber* buried at increasing depths. The most promising trainees can take advantage of a kind of postgraduate course, taking part in simulated truffle hunts organized by the industrious Monchiero family for tourists, mostly non-Italians, who have great fun following the rummagings of Black, Mirka, Lady, Titti et al.

A trained dog is worth thousands of euros, and Baròt IV recalls that his grandfather sold one to an emissary of Joe Di Maggio. The American baseball champion, born in California to immigrants from Palermo, was also famous for having briefly been married to Marilyn Monroe, to whom Giacomo Morra sent a enormous truffle in 1954.

Chapter 3

Discovering the Alba White

Truffles in Pre-Unification Piedmont

Particularly in the 18th century, Piedmont and the Savoy dynasty played an important role in raising the profile of the white truffle.
Frequently served during banquets, the underground fungi appear in 18th-century culinary treatises and cookbooks, though the name of the species is rarely given. Intense scientific curiosity developed around truffles, with their still unclear botanical classification and mysterious reproduction. The idea of hunting truffles with dogs appealed to the foreign ambassadors at the court, and people began to wonder if white truffles grew in other countries. In 1723, the French king, Louis XV, asked his grandfather, Vittorio Amedeo II of Savoy, to send him an expert hunter and some dogs. In 1751, a similar request arrived from the British court, specifically from Prince William, Duke of Cumberland, the son of George II. In response, Carlo Emanuele III sent seven trained dogs, handled by the truffle-hunting Vanchina brothers.[1]
Truffles were also being dispatched. Evidence comes from a letter sent in 1782 by Vittorio Alfieri, an Asti-born writer and nobleman. Writing from Rome to his sister Giulia, he complained that his truffles had arrived half crushed and spoiled because they had not been properly packed. "When packing them, they must be immobilized in bran," recommends Alfieri, continuing: "in fact the other years they arrived in excellent condition." Even back in 1380, the Savoia-Acaias were sending truffles to Bonne of Bourbon,[2] the wife of the Green Count,

X
FIERA DEL TARTUFO

Amedeo VI, while in 1814 Louis XVIII asked if he could again receive truffles from Piedmont like in the days before the French Revolution.[3]

In 1776, the Canavese abbot Giovanni Bernardo Vigo, a teacher of Latin rhetoric at the University of Turin and imitator of Virgil, published a short didactic poem in Latin and Italian, *Tubera terrae*,[4] which offers a detailed description of where and when truffles are found, the different types of terrain, truffle varieties, the use and training of dogs, theories about truffle reproduction, their use in the kitchen and how to store them. The truffle landscape identified by Vigo is undoubtedly that of the Langhe and Monferrato, even if the first name is absent from the description, which refers to "the slopes of the Ligurian mountains covered in vines and woods, and the Tanaro and the Bormida with the valleys carved out by their rapid waters, and the beautiful hills dear to Bacchus and Ceres that rise around Asti, mother of illustrious men, and those of Monferrato."[5] Equally interesting are his thoughts on the gastronomic value of *Tubera terrae*: "What to say of the innumerable dishes, which thanks to truffles acquire the best flavour? Who could enumerate them quickly? Without them, the wealth of banquets is not sumptuous enough, and the same opulence does not fully satisfy." Vigo also shares the tricks used by truffle consumers to clean the fungi: "first they scrape off the dirt, then they sprinkle them with warm water and rub them with a small brush." To cut the truffles, they use a *rasiera*, very similar to our modern-day truffle shaver, a blade held by a thin piece of walnut wood, designed to shave the truffle into thin slices and not yet known to the common people.[6]

In 1780, the Polish count Michel-Jean de Borch, an erudite globe-trotter, gourmet and amateur naturalist, published a collection of letters[7] he had sent to Piedmontese nobles on the subject

of Piedmontese truffles: white (at the time called grey), bianchetto and black. He describes their characteristics, their appearance under the microscope and his experiments with cultivation, and claims to have managed to reproduce the white truffle. His opinion about the superior quality of the region's truffles is clear: "Does someone say that in Richmond Park [in London, *ed.*] they find truffles with the same fragrance as those from Piedmont? I think I can cast doubt on such a claim, because we have not yet seen in any part of Europe a product equal to those from certain Piedmontese provinces." [8]
In 1788, the Turinese Vittorio Pico wrote a lengthy work in Latin to obtain admission to his city's College of Medicine.[9] Discoursing on the nature and classification of the fungi and their effects on the human body, he identified four truffle varieties, including *Tuber magnatum* (from *magnatium*, meaning of the rich, the lords, the powerful). With reference to the botanical studies of his fellow citizen Carlo Ludovico Allioni,[10] chief medical examiner of Vittorio Amedeo III, Pico describes the truffle "of the lords" as being "of irregular shape, externally yellowish grey, delicate to the touch, with very pale white-grey flesh, elegantly interlaced by veins of snake-like colour, often marked by reddish blotches here and there. An autumnal product with a delicious smell and taste, peculiar to the Monferrato, the area around Asti and the Ligurian hills [another name for the Langhe at the time, *ed.*]." He adds that the truffles of this species "in the vernacular are given the generic name of *Trifole*, to which some add *Grise* [grey]."[11]
With his acclaimed degree thesis, Doctor Pico earned the honour of having his surname forever associated with the official names of the fungi he classified as *Tuber magnatum* and *T. albidum*. About 40 years later, the latter, commonly known in Italy as bianchetto or

marzuolo, was given the parallel name of *T. borchii*, in tribute to pioneer Michel-Jean de Borch, by Carlo Vittadini. The doctor and mycologist from Lombardy was the author of fundamental texts, including the description,[12] illustrated with coloured plates of his own drawings, of 65 truffle ecotypes, around 50 of which were entirely new. Vittadini (often abbreviated Vittad. or Vitt.), gave his name to many species of truffle, including six of the nine that are allowed to be collected and sold in Italy: as well as *Tuber borchii* (a synonym of *T. albidum* Pico) also *T. melanosporum, aestivum, brumale, macrosporum* and *mesentericum*. *Tuber uncinatum* and *T. brumale moscatum* were instead catalogued in the last decade of the 19th century by Gaspar Adolphe Chatin (1813-1901) and René Joseph Justin Ferry (1845-1924), both from France.

Meanwhile, in his *Physiology of Taste*, published in Paris in 1825,[13] the magistrate and gourmet Jean-Anthelme Brillat-Savarin dedicated a whole chapter to truffles, whose consumption had grown compared to the previous century and which were in great fashion as he was writing. "The meal is almost unknown in which no truffled dish occurs", he writes. After a disquisition on their digestibility and debatable aphrodisiac effects, he concludes: "The truffle is not a positive aphrodisiac, but it can upon occasion make women tenderer and men more apt to love." He continues: "White truffles are found in Piedmont, of extreme merit; they have a faint taste of garlic, which mars their perfection not at all, being free from unpleasing after-effects."[14]

The most celebrated Piedmontese chef of the 19th century was Giovanni Vialardi (1804-1872), from Biella, first assistant and then head chef at the Savoy court under Carlo Alberto and Vittorio Emanuele II. After publishing a treatise on cooking, in 1863 he came out with a book destined for great success, *Cucina borghese*

semplice ed economica[15] (*Simple and Affordable Middle-Class Cooking*), which contained a certain number of recipes using truffles, both black and white, testifying to their widespread use. White truffles are used in remarkable quantities with eggs, risotto, polenta, chicken, guinea hen and pheasant, in a sauce for cardoons and as a filling for a pie, cut into thin shavings and sometimes even cooked, at odds with contemporary usage and undoubtedly jeopardizing their fragrance and flavour.

---

1. *Tubera terrae carmen Johannis Bernardi Vigi rhetoricae professoris - I tartufi, poemetto di Giambernardo Vigo professor di rettorica tradotto dal latino*, Stamperia Reale, Turin 1776, p.IXX; republished, with a preface by Mario Soldati and an introduction by Franco Montacchini, in the Italian translation by Maria Cristina Bogliolo, from Nexus, Borgosesia 1994. Cited in Enrico Vigna, *Trifulau e tartufi. Aspetti antropologici dell'economia rurale tra Langhe e Monferrato*, University of Genoa-Province of Asti, Brigati, Genoa 1999.
2. Cf. Franco Montacchini, introduction to *I tartufi / Giovanni Bernardo Vigo*, op.cit., p.18.
3. On the Savoy habit of sending gifts of truffles to the major European courts, as well as dogs accompanied by expert truffle hunters, with the aim of extending the search for the precious underground fungi to other countries, cf. Domenico Perrero, "I regali di prodotti nazionali invalsi nella diplomazia piemontese dei secoli 17° e 18°", extracted from *Atti della Regia Accademia delle Scienze*, vol. 31, Clausen, Turin 1896.
4. *Tubera terrae carmen Johannis Bernardi Vigi*... and *Tubera terrae: carmen... - I tartufi / Giovanni Bernardo Vigo*, op.cit.; Maria Cristina Albonico, *I tartufi di Giovanni Bernardo Vigo*, Aracne, Rome 2007. A dialect version of the text

also exists: G.B. Vigo, O. Gallina, "La trifola", in *Almanacco piemontese di vita e cultura*, Viglongo, Turin 1975.

5 Giovanni Bernardo Vigo, *I tartufi*, Nexus, Borgosesia 1994; translation by Maria Cristina Bogliolo. Cf. Davide Bobba, "La natura come risorsa: boschi e corsi d'acqua delle Langhe", in *Le Langhe di Camillo Cavour. Dai feudi all'Italia unita*, Skira, Milan 2011, p.149. This book contains a huge amount of information of great help when reconstructing the history of southern Piedmont; it is the catalogue of an exhibition held from 18 June to 13 November, 2011, in Alba, at the Palazzo Mostre e Congressi "Giacomo Morra", on the initiative of the Fondazione Cassa di Risparmio di Cuneo, the City of Alba, Fondazione Piera, Pietro and Giovanni Ferrero and the Piedmont Regional Authority, as part of the celebrations for the 150th anniversary of Italian Unification.

6. *Ibid.*, p.149.

7. Michel-Jean de Borch, *Lettres sur les truffes du Piémont*, Frères Reycends, Milan 1780; anastatic printing and Italian translation in 1,000 numbered copies, Ordine dei Cavalieri del Tartufo e dei Vini di Alba, Alba 1974.

8. Cited by Sandro Doglio in *Dizionario di gastronomia del Piemonte*, Daumerie, Montiglio 1995.

9. *Victorii Pici phil. et medic. doctoris taurinensis ampliss. Medicorum collegii candidati Melethemata inauguralia. De fungorum generatione et propagatione*, Giammichele Briolo, Turin 1788.

10. *Flora Pedemontana sive enumeratio methodica stirpium indigenarum Pedemontii auctore Carolo Allionio... Tomus primus [-tertius]*, Giammichele Briolo, Turin 1785; *Flora pedemontana / Carlo Allioni*, anastatic reproduction in 2 volumes, Olschki, Florence 2003.

11. *Victorii Pici phil. et medic. doctoris taurinensis...*, op.cit., p.79. Cf. Davide Bobba, "La natura come risorsa...", op.cit., p.149.

12. Carolo Vittadini, *Monographia Tuberacearum*, F. Rusconi, Milan 1831; Carlo Vittadini, *Funghi ipogei: Monographia Tuberacearum*, translation by Giacomo Lazzari and anastatic reproduction of the original text with coloured plates; [followed by] *Tartufi del Cantone Ticino*, Società micologica Carlo Benzoni, Chiasso 1991.

13. Jean-Anthelme Brillat-Savarin, *Physiologie du gout ou méditations de gastronomie transcendante*, Paulin, Paris 1846 (1826); English edition, *The Physiology of Taste*, Dover, Mineola NY 2002.

14. Brillat-Savarin, op.cit., *Méditation VI*, II.43-44.

15. *Cucina borghese semplice ed economica / per Giovanni Vialardi*, G. Favale and C., Turin 1863; anastatic reprinting Forni, Sala Bolognese 2009.

* Genoa Is Worth A Truffle

New information about the use of truffles as a "diplomatic weapon" was recently discovered by Giordano Berti, the curator of the Historic Truffle Archive.

According to a biographer of the Savoys, at an official lunch organized during the Congress of Verona in 1822, the king of Sardinia, Carlo Felice of Savoy (1765-1831), was given the honour of sitting in front of Tsar Alexander, Emperor of all the Russias. This privilege, writes the biographer, was the result of having brought from Piedmont "certain truffles that gave Alexander great pleasure and awakened in him certain forgotten cravings". During the lunch, the emperor, addressing the Savoy sovereign, expressed his gratitude for the gesture and assured him of his desire to confirm "that to your ancient states should be added the superb Genoa", as had been decided during the Congress of Vienna in 1815. In regards to truffles, it seems the emperor said to King Carlo Felice: "I never feel so free from boredom as when I eat them; I feel that vivacity, that agility that they say is innate to the birds".

Italy's Leading Truffle Fairs

The original meaning of the Italian *fiera* was a regular market generally held on holy days, *feriae* in Latin. The concept has evolved over the centuries, and *fiera* is now used to refer to a large exhibition-market held regularly in a specific place and focused on one or more production sectors (and, slightly improperly, to a local folk festival, also known as a *sagra*).
Among these specialist fairs, those dedicated to truffles are of considerable importance. Leaving aside festivals and *sagre*, which are different and do not require regional recognition, in Italy there are around 60 truffle fairs, of which only one is international (for white truffles, held in Alba, in the Piedmontese province of Cuneo, on the weekends between the middle of October and the middle of November). Of the others, 20 are national and the rest regional or local.
In Piedmont, national fairs are held in Cortemilia (province of Cuneo); Montechiaro d'Asti and Moncalvo (province of Asti); Murisengo and San Sebastiano Curone (province of Alessandria) and Rivalba (province of Turin, known as the Turinese Hills White Truffle Fair). In Liguria, one is held in Millesimo, and Emilia-Romagna has the Fragno a Calestano Black Truffle Fair (province of Parma) and a fair for white truffles in Sant'Agata Feltria (province of Rimini). Tuscany has the San Miniato White Truffle Fair (province of Pisa), now in its 44th edition. The Norcia Black Truffle Fair (province of Perugia), between February and March, has been held for over 50 years, and is the most important

of Umbria's national fairs. The others are in Gubbio, Città di Castello and Valtopina (all in the province of Perugia) and Fabro (province of Terni). Three national fairs, all dedicated to the white truffle, are held in the Marche province of Pesaro and Urbino: a recently established one in Pergola and two historic fairs, both around 50 years old, in Acqualagna and Sant'Angelo in Vado. In Lazio, the Ciociaria truffle festivals have merged into the national fairs for white, black and (in June) scorzone truffles in Campoli Appennino (province of Frosinone). For some years now in Molise, the fairs organized in San Pietro Avellana (province of Isernia) have been joined by the national Molise White Truffle Fair, held in December in the provincial capital of Isernia. The list of Italy's national fairs, from north to south, concludes with the Colliano Truffle and Typical Local Food Fair in the province of Salerno, in the Campania region.

The Acqualagna Fair

A small town with a population of around 4,500 in the Marche province of Pesaro and Urbino, Acqualagna is positioned along the ancient Via Fano-Furlo Pass stretch of the Roman consular road linking Rimini to Rome, the Via Flaminia. It is also one of the capitals for the white truffle, whose historic denominations are in fact "Alba white truffle" and "Acqualagna white truffle". Truffles have traditionally been gathered and sold here for centuries, making it a privileged place for the promotion and sale of both the most prized of underground fungi and the other types of truffle that are collected or cultivated (black truffles) locally. Total annual production is around 60,000 kilos.
During their respective seasons, regional festivals in Acqualagna celebrate *Tuber melanosporum* and *T. aestivum*, the summer truffle or scorzone, but

the most important event is the National White Truffle Fair, held between October and November. In recent years an average of over 200,000 visitors have attended each edition. The heart of the fair is the Palatartufo, 4,000 square metres for buying and sampling all kinds of *T. magnatum* products, as well as other specialties, mostly local but also from elsewhere in Italy. The Salotto da Gustare, meanwhile, offers attractions such as guided tastings, demonstrations by famous chefs, celebrity cooking challenges and book presentations.

The International Alba Fair

Alba, a city of 31,000 inhabitants in the northeast corner of the southern Piedmontese province of Cuneo, is the administrative centre for the hilly district of the Langhe and Roero. Every autumn since 1928, it hosts a white truffle fair, officially international since 2007, and one of Italy's oldest events. According to a recent study by the Fitzcarraldo Foundation, promoted by the CRC Foundation (*Gli eventi fieristici come fattori di sviluppo in provincia di Cuneo*, 2013), one out of every four visitors comes from outside of Italy, and two out of three are from outside Piedmont.

The fair is currently held over six weekends, from the second week of October to the third week of November. A mix of food and wine, folklore, culture and sport, at the centre of everything is the immense truffle market, guaranteeing the highest quality and a wide selection, surrounded by stands representing other Piedmontese foods. Over the years, new activities have been added, like sensory analysis sessions and a mock truffle hunt, tastings of the Langhe and Roero's great wines and winery visits, plus tastings and seminars focused on PGI Piedmont hazelnuts, the province of Cuneo's artisanal chocolate and the region's PDO cheeses. Not to mention cooking demonstrations from the many renowned local chefs, local food markets like the Earth Market organized in collaboration with Slow Food Italy and Coldiretti's Campagna Amica. Another mainstay of the fair is the series of medieval re-enactments, with performances and food tastings in the city's streets and piazzas and the Donkey Palio. Cultural events (exhibitions, concerts, readings) are concentrated during the fair and throughout the autumn, as are sporting competitions, from the Barbaresco and Truffle Marathon to golf tournaments.

The fair's fame has also grown thanks to its awarding of the Truffle of the Year to an international or Italian personality. Celebrities who have visited Alba to collect their award include Gérard Depardieu, Sophia Loren, Alain Delon, Claudia Cardinale, Luciano Pavarotti, Marcello Lippi, Sting, Prince Albert of Monaco, Francis Ford Coppola and Penélope Cruz. The International Truffle Auction, a charity event brilliantly conceived by Bruno Ceretto, also brings the world's attention to Alba. Held in November in the Grinzane Cavour castle, it is organized by the Cavour Regional Enoteca, the Association of Alba Shopkeepers, the Truffle Study Centre and the Piedmont Regional Authority. In past editions, bidders from Paris, Moscow, Las Vegas, London, Munich, Tokyo, New York, Los Angeles, Hollywood and Hong Kong have been connected live to the auction.

* The Donkey Palio and the Joust of the Hundred Towers

Initially it was a light-hearted prank, the result of the idle chatter of a fun-loving group who enlivened the provincial peace and quiet of Alba in the 1930s, frequenting the Savona's café, restaurant and Tavernetta and in the summer organizing gleeful food-filled excursions along the Tanaro. But among the originators of the playful parody of Asti's Palio horse race was a certain Giuseppe Gallizio (1902-1964), a great enthusiast of folk festivals and the traditional ballgame pallone elastico. A chemist and pharmacist by trade, he belatedly discovered a host of other vocations: for archaeology, for medicinal and aromatic herbs (he shared his knowledge as a teacher at the Alba Enological School and the Agriculture Faculty of the University of Turin), for fighting against the fascists (an active partisan, he was a member of the Committee of National Liberation, and a municipal councillor after the liberation) and lastly – following an encounter with Piero Simondo of Turin, a student of Felice Casorati's at the Accademia Albertina – as a painter. In this last guise he became Pinot Gallizio, founder of the first experimental laboratory for an Imaginist Bauhaus in Alba in 1955. The following year he convened the First World Congress of Free Artists, and in 1957, at Simondo's birthplace, Cosio di Arroscia, near Imperia, he was one of the founders of the Situationist International. Its members included Guy Debord, Asger Jorn, Michèle Bernstein and Ralph Rumney. But back when the Truffle Fair was started, Gallizio was not yet an artist moving in international circles, universally known as the inventor of "industrial painting". He was a young man who enjoyed having fun, always on the hunt for new entertainment opportunities with his companions in revelry. He and his friends "wanted to take part in the Asti Palio to create excuses for discussion and entertainment", wrote Antonio Buccolo and Giulio Parusso in *Alba: il Palio* (photographs by Enrico Necade, Famija Albeisa 1987). "The invitation was forever promised, but never forthcoming. Out of this

came the idea of organizing a Palio in Alba, and as they evidently couldn't count on a supply of horses, they fell back on donkeys: less paraphernalia, a longer race and more guaranteed and popular amusement." Asti, home to a historic Palio, had always been Alba's main rival. According to the chronicles, on 10 August, 1275 — the feast day of San Lorenzo, Alba's patron saint – the Astigiani troops stopped the Angevin invaders, Alba's allies, on their way to the Colle di Tenda pass. The Astigiani, allied under the circumstances with the Monferrato marquessate, mockingly ran their Palio — already a tradition in honour of their patron saint, San Secondo – under the partially destroyed walls of the enemy city, Alba. Suggesting the replacement of horses with donkeys was a benign way of teasing Alba's historic adversaries.

Alba's first donkey race was held in Piazza San Giovanni as part of the 1932 Truffle Fair. For the occasion, the city was divided into six *borghi* (districts), each headed by a *borgomastro* who chose the jockey. The winner was the

rider recruited by the Borgo dei Postiglioni (the railway station neighbourhood), atop an ass called Tren, who trounced his competitors the following years as well.
Despite the great popularity of the event and the interest it inspired, including mentions in the national press, after just three editions the Palio was suspended. It was brought back in the immediate post-war period, thanks to a committee presided over by Dr Tommaso Vico, the Truffle Fair president and the son of Giovanni Vico, also a doctor and the pre- and anti-fascist mayor of Alba. In 1951 it was decided to give the race a new boost by reviving the borghi and involving the surrounding villages in the event, which was renamed the *Giostra delle Cento Torri* ("joust of the hundred towers"), recalling Alba's glorious past, but this attempt was short lived.
The Palio was again put on hold until 1967, when three members of the Truffle Fair committee, Paolo Farinetti, Adolfo Barbero and Carlo Aimeri, had the idea of restoring the donkey race, this time setting up the racetrack around the cathedral and accompanying the race

with magnificent costumed re-enactments of medieval life: the Giostra delle Cento Torri. "The organizers' enthusiasm infected the city," recalls Giulio Parusso in *Tartufo* (St Pauls International, Alba 2012). "Wherever there was a bar, a borgo would be started, with its committee [...]; others set up headquarters in private homes [...]. Twelve Borghi took part in the Giostra, the highest number yet; three heats were held with four donkeys each, and the top two went through to the final [...]; after leading the way the whole race, Borgo del Fumo's Ringo pulled up halfway across the finishing line and there was no way of moving him until Caterina, from the Borgo *dij Sagrin* [of sorrows, *ed.*], passed him, winning the Palio."
This is the donkey race that has survived to the present day, weathering criticism from animal rights

activists. Every year, the race is accompanied by a more spectacular Giostra, with a huge number of characters, flag wavers, musicians and so on. The investiture of the Podestà, who for the duration of the Truffle Fair serves as the lord of Alba, is followed by an evocative procession in period costume of ladies and knights, noblemen and commoners, merchants and soldiers, accompanied by trumpet blasts and drumrolls. During the weekends, episodes from the city's history are performed, mixing reality and fantasy. During the *Festa dei Nove Borghi*, the feast of the nine districts, hundreds of costumed extras distribute typical foods, organize traditional games and play music, mixing with the crowd of visitors to sing and dance. The jolly fellows of the 1930s would have enjoyed this cheerful festival, particularly Pinot, who watches over the Palio in spirit, particularly since 1981, when it was decided to give a different painter every year the task of decorating the cloth presented to the winning borgo. These days, the artist is chosen in agreement with the Truffle Fair's organizers and the Giostra delle Cento Torri. Some of the artists have been nationally renowned, while others are known more locally; some have already made a name for themselves, while others are just starting out. In 2008, it was the turn of Piero Simondo, in his 80s, while for the 2012 Palio they used a canvas by Gallizio, the pharmacist-alchemist turned industrial painter who sat at the Savona's tables, participating with equal enthusiasm in silly jokes and in learned discussions with teachers from the Govone school – the existentialist philosopher Pietro Chiodi, the literature master Leonardo Cocito, anti-fascist teachers from Fenoglio's generation – or, with due reverence, with the rector of the Diocesan Seminary, Natale Bussi and the "bishop of the partisans" Luigi Maria Grassi.

Perhaps destiny had a hand in the fact that within a few months, between 1963 and 1964, Alba lost three of the heroes of an extraordinary season in the life of a provincial city: Beppe Fenoglio, in his 40s, Pinot Gallizio, in his 60s, and Giacomo Morra, in his 70s. An unrepeatable season, echoed faintly but still comfortingly every October in Alba.

From 1928 to the Present

The original germ of the Truffle Fair was the spectacular exhibition-market organized by Giacomo Morra in front his already-celebrated hotel and restaurant, Savona, as part of the celebrations to mark the end of the 1928 grape harvest. The following year, the market was organized with the official collaboration of the municipal authority, separated from the grape-harvest festival and named the Trade Fair with Prizes for Renowned Langhe Truffles. In 1930, the event's incredible success, with floods of visitors arriving on special trains from Turin, prompted the establishment of a committee to organize future editions. It was presided over by parliamentarian Gastone Guerrieri, the count of Mirafiori and Fontanafredda, nephew to Vittorio Emanuele II and Rosa Vercellana (La Bela Rosin) and therefore King Vittorio Emanuele III's morganatic cousin.

He was certainly the most powerful figure in the province, and we have an almost first-hand account of his role in the origins of the Truffle Fair, recorded over 60 years ago by Raoul Molinari, at the time a youthful habitué of the Savona as well as Morra's ghostwriter. His friend Giordano Berti printed the story in the entertaining book *Il re del tartufo* (Araba Fenice, Boves 2011). According to Molinari, who was present at the interview, in November 1952 the restaurateur related the precise circumstances surrounding the fair's creation to American journalist Robert Littell. It was the 15th of August, 1928, and a diverse trio of diners was seated at one of the Savona's tables: the doctor Giovanni Vico, former mayor of Alba; lawyer Giulio Cesare Moreno, Alba's incumbent podestà (magistrate); and Gastone di

Mirafiori. An abundant truffle harvest was predicted, thanks to the summer's heavy rainfall. Morra had come up with the idea of organizing a truffle market that autumn, and he shared it during the usual chat with his distinguished clients over dessert. He received the count's immediate consent and full support.

Apart from this story, which seems reliably accurate, it is known that Mirafiori – a great landowner and winegrower, member of parliament since 1913, senator of the realm since 1934, president of the Provincial Economic Council and close relative of the Savoys – was from the start one of the leading "sponsors" of the Truffle Fair. Perhaps it was an entrepreneurial sixth sense which unfortunately failed him in other situations, or perhaps he was looking for new spaces of consensus, competing with his main rivals within

the government, both from Asti: Pietro Badoglio, the army's chief of general staff, and Vincenzo Buronzo, an intellectual and veteran politician, held to be very powerful because he was the brother-in-law of one of il Duce's sons, Arnaldo Mussolini. With the same intensity with which he had pleaded the case of Alba's law court, abolished in 1924 and re-established in 1932, Mirafiori took on the role of promoter and, from 1930, also organizer of the Truffle Fair. His name undoubtedly brought lustre and fame to the event. This is easily confirmed by the documented presence of notable figures at the fair's inaugural ceremonies: for example, the heir to the throne, Prince Umberto, in 1936. But the invitations to the bigwigs of the day almost always received a positive response even after the fall of the regime, when, following the end of its "23 days"* and the war, a democratic Alba brought back the custom of the fair. "Two things were never lacking: the speeches and the ribbon-cutting", writes Giulio Parusso in *Tartufo* (St Pauls International, Alba 2012).

"The former were always an opportunity to underline the local problems and ask for their resolution, often in vain, despite ministerial promises. The ribbon-cutting was primarily for the photographers and also to allow the various politicians who had spoken and all those who believed themselves important to elbow their way forward to get close to the VIP who was opening the fair."

Parusso continues: "In the first years of the Truffle Fair, the presence of representatives from the House of Savoy and the government was much sought-after. The habit of inviting undersecretaries and ministers was immediately picked up again after the war, almost always with success, with even the very impressive attendance of prime ministers like Giovanni Goria and Giulio Andreotti. [...] There were also unexpected and enjoyable surprises and particularly significant inaugurations. In 1992, after the ribbon-cutting and tour of the pavilions, the American ambassador, Peter Secchia, expressed a desire to visit the fun fair, and everyone ended up on the rollercoaster. In 1993, in tribute to the twinned cities and, above all, the German tourists who visited the area in such droves, the fair was opened by the mayor of Böblingen, Alexander Vogelgsang, and simultaneously by representatives from the state of Israel and Arafat's PLO, sealing the peace deal which had recently been signed and had now been underlined by Alba white truffles." Even back then, the "provincial" city of Alba's fair was clearly "international".

* Beppe Fenoglio's first book, published in 1952, is a collection of short stories about partisans fighting against fascism during the war, *I ventitré giorni della città di Alba* (*The 23 Days of the City of Alba*). The title refers to when 2,000 partisans took the city from the Fascists in October 1944, holding it under siege for 23 days before it was recaptured.

⁂ The Father of Alba Truffles

"The many anecdotes from [Giacomo Morra's] life make it easy to define him a character. Throughout his life he was interviewed, visited, quoted, sought out and honoured more than any other Albese of his time. At the tables of his kingdom sat not only the biggest names in show business, but also politicians, writers, businessmen, an endless number of gourmets and gastronomes, tourists from all over the world and hundreds of thousands of diners drawn by his personality, the fragrance of truffles, the great wines of Alba, the mythical name of his Savona and the creations of its kitchen, which offered long-forgotten dishes from Alba's traditional cuisine.

In the catering field, he was uniquely able to create a cooking school based on practical training, made up of a lengthy *stage*, during which a cook won their certificate and diploma by working in the kitchen. This school produced a number of legendary chefs who worked in the area's prestigious restaurants and famous trattorias for over 50 years.

His concern for quality ingredients led him to start a farm in the Vaccheria plain to grow his own vegetables, to raise pigs and cows, to start a winery [...] and to enlist hunters to bring him hares, pheasants, quails and partridges. [...] When it came to truffles, he was the first to grasp all the fascination they could inspire and their promotional potential for a city, Alba, and an area, the Langhe, and for the other fruits of the land: wine, meat, hazelnuts and nougat, cheeses. [...]

In 1928, he acquired the Savona hotel [...] and put all of his efforts into a restoration that was quite exceptional for the time [...] and opened up the bar, billiard room, dance hall and restaurant not just to hotel guests but to the whole city. It soon became an essential point of reference in Alba, a meeting place for wine producers, grape growers, brokers and salesmen and a location for banquets for the Alba community. Morra also provided catering services for special occasions with large numbers of guests.

In the field of promotion, he came up with the idea of the Truffle Fair, and supported it financially until the end of his life. He would spend hours in a little salon on the first

floor discussing it with Count Gastone of Mirafiori [...] In the period after the Second World War, Giacomo Morra came up with the idea of presenting the year's biggest truffle to an international celebrity, and when he sent a truffle weighing 2,520 grams to the US president, Harry Truman, the news made headlines around the world. To satisfy the curiosity of tourists and journalists, he expanded the Truffle Dog University in Roddi, a canine training school, and promoted the idea of mock truffle hunts, leaving the real quest to a happy few.
[...] As a hotelier he was always courteous and available [...] He was a restaurateur with great insight, inventing an infinite variety of antipasti; and also a dealer in black truffles as well as white, sourced from Norcia and sold to the French. He even found a system for preserving them, and in 1948 was selling his fresh and preserved truffles in the United States. He was known as the King of Truffles, and his sons Mario, Giorgio and Francesco continued his dynasty and his businesses until the 1990s."

Beppe Fenoglio Literature, History, Art and Culture Study Centre Association
www.centrostudibeppefenoglio.it

At the Savona the World

"In his restaurant, the legendary Savona, Morra offered a highly refined gastronomy, a mix of Savoy cuisine and Langhe tradition, whose principal ingredient was the white truffle. Workers and professionals, farmers and politicians, industrialists and the international jet set: they could all sit at the Savona's tables. A dance hall was opened in the basement, the Tavernetta, where Italy's most famous orchestras played. A real truffle industry started up in the back of the restaurant, comparable to other flourishing local enterprises: the chocolates of Ferrero, the textiles of Miroglio...
In the 1950s, Morra earned the title of King of Truffles, gifting extraordinary examples of the precious fungus to celebrities around the world: American presidents Harry Truman, Ike Eisenhower and John F. Kennedy; the head of the Kremlin, Nikita Khrushchev; actresses Rita Hayworth and Marilyn Monroe; British statesman Winston Churchill and Ethiopian emperor Haile Selassie.
Myriad personalities gravitated around the 'palace' of the King of Truffles: philosophers, artists, musicians, ordinary people. It was at the Savoy restaurant that Alfred Hitchcock planned the script for a thriller set in the Langhe. Situationist Pinot Gallizio came up with the idea of canning the odour of Alba and exporting it around the world. Federico Rossano wrote the Hymn to the Truffle. The Gypsy Bacci created an improbable truffled elixir of love. The ex-monarch of Egypt, Farouk, arrived with a lavish retinue to sample what was known as the cooking of the king."

Giordano Berti, Raoul Molinari, *Il re del tartufo*, Araba Fenice, Boves 2011

A White Truffle for the White House

Over two and half kilos. To be precise, 2,520 grams. That was the weight of the *Tuber magnatum* Pico which in autumn 1951 Giacomo Morra, following an appropriate publicity build-up, sent to the United States president, Harry Truman. After all, he said, "the world's biggest truffle should go to the world's most powerful man."

The Korean War had broken out the year before, and Truman had ordered restrictions on overseas travel for American citizens, wrecking the enterprising restaurateur's plans to participate in a project to convert a large Vatican-owned palazzo in Rome into a place to receive the crowds of pilgrims expected to arrive from abroad for the Jubilee. Donating the best truffle ever dug out of the depths of the earth to the president was the equivalent of saying to the Americans: "You can't come to Italy? You're worried about your boys on the front and a possible nuclear escalation of the conflict? Well, as a sign of affinity and solidarity we're sending you the best thing we have." By sending the truffle to the White House's current occupant, Morra was symbolically sending it to all Americans, including a certain J. Edward Cardigan, who from Rochester, Monroe County, New York, had sent him a cheque for five dollars in return for "a box of equal value of the exquisite fruits which I ate in slices over spaghetti [i.e. *tajarin*, *ed.*] when I passed through Alba

in 1946 when I was a sergeant in the US Army".

Many years later, in November 2006, interviewed by a journalist from the newspaper *Il Tirreno*, one of the sons of the great Giacomo, the then 87-year-old Francesco Morra, told the back story behind the operation: "Tuscan truffles had nothing to do with that one weighing 2 kilos and 520 grams which my father gave to President Truman. It was found by a farmer from Novello, who begged us not to reveal where he'd found it, for fear that others would go hunting there. We sent it to the White House through a cousin of ours who worked for Rai [the state broadcaster, *ed.*] in Turin." But, wondered the interviewer, did the colossus reach its destination? "Apparently so, because a few days later the CIA contacted us: they wanted to make sure that big smelly potato hadn't gone bad. In any case it must have been eaten and appreciated, because then Truman's entourage asked for others, which of course we made them pay for."

An American at the Court of King Giacomo

"A pilgrimage to the Piedmont [...] begins in the pleasant market town of Alba, specifically at the Grand Hotel Restaurant Savona. Here its owners, the Morra family, father and sons, buy, sell, serve, eat, can, export, and otherwise stimulate truffles. Here the Truffle King himself, Signor Giacomo Morra, an ancient, bald, and bony man with eyes glittering behind steel spectacles, showed us a prize truffle just about to be airmailed to Uruguay. It was a collection of rooty, loam-colored bulges, a shapeless shape about the size of a soccer ball. We were allowed to feel it, reverently, and sniff it. The scent of an untamed white truffle, even when sniffed out of doors where it cannot gather momentum, does not suggest feasts in three-starred restaurants. It smells of earth or rather of dark depths that have never been ploughed, of subsoil. To the Morras, and to all right-thinking people of Alba and the district, it is a lovely, an intoxicating, and above all a prosperous odor."

Robert Littell, "School for Truffle Hounds", originally published in *Reader's Digest*, republished in *It Takes All Kinds*, Reynal, New York 1961

The "Truffle District" Takes Shape

In 1963, a few days before Christmas, Giacomo Morra unexpectedly passed away. It was a great loss to Alba, to the Langhe, to the Truffle Fair he had "invented" and to the white truffle he had made famous around the world. But luckily the great Giacomo had worthy spiritual heirs, in addition to the sons who continued his businesses for three decades. On the surface, the most madcap was Raoul Molinari, who served as press secretary (as we would call it now) for Morra. He ran the Truffle Fair in the 1970s, bringing in a host of innovations: highlighting the event's local character, firmly linking promotion of the truffle with the Langhe and Roero's other typical products – first and foremost the great wines, which were taking their first steps towards DOC classification – the relaunch of traditional cuisine, the boost for the restaurants who best interpreted it, the development of side initiatives. But all of this, particularly in regards to food and wine – which played its part in the recognition of the fair's national status in 1973 – was made possible to a great extent by the codification and communication developed by the Famija Albeisa and the Ordine dei Cavalieri del Tartufo di Alba (Order of the Knights of the Alba Truffle), both presided over by pharmacist, winegrower and gourmet Luciano Degiacomi. In more official roles – as chairman of the Alba Bra Langhe Roero consortium, which organized the Truffle Fair from 1996 to 2003, and of the Cuneo Chamber of Commerce – his colleague Giacomo Oddero continued his work. A tireless promoter of the province of Cuneo's gastronomic specialties, between 1996 and 2000 he was the driving force behind the creation of the National Truffle Study Centre. In 2007, given the intense activity being carried in the field of sensory analysis by the Study Centre, and the considerable number of judges who had been trained in all the truffle-producing regions,

Oddero championed the formation of the International Organization of Truffle Tasters. The organization's members are involved in truffle sensory analysis as a quality control method, a support for scientific research and an opportunity for education and in training new judges and running refresher courses.

In 2003, the municipal authority set up the Ente Fiera Nazionale del Tartufo Bianco d'Alba, the National Alba White Truffle Fair Organizing Committee, made up of the municipality, the Association of Alba Shopkeepers and the Giostra delle Cento Torri. Chaired first by Alberto Cirio and then Antonio Degiacomi, it organizes both the Truffle Fair and other events in the city. The emphasis is on international promotion, helped by the active collaboration of wine producers, both big and small. A generation of restaurateurs who pursue research as well as tradition is growing in number and quality. Other chefs are settling here, attracted by the area's growth in winemaking and tourism, not to mention the fame and fascination of the truffle. The gifts of nature have been joined by a coordinated ensemble of professional skills, from hunting to selection to marketing, from cooking to hospitality to tourist services, forming a genuine "truffle district".

International At Last

A study carried out by Unioncamere in 2006 concluded that the Alba Truffle Fair is the best-known food and wine event in Italy. The year after came the long-awaited recognition as officially international. As Valentina Montisci writes in the conclusion to the detailed chronology in the appendix of the book *Alba e la Fiera del Tartufo* (photographs by Silvia Muratore and Bruno Murialdo, text by Luigi Sugliano, Sorì, Piobesi d'Alba 2007), the Truffle Fair is also "culture, spectacle, escapism, reflection, the story of a land, a means of promotion. A grand, beautiful and generous story, constructed by the city of Alba and its people."

Chapter 4

Protecting Truffles

€ 400,00 per hg
provenienza: Piemonte · Italia

Consumer Protection

Truffles, particularly the prized black and white varieties, and even more particularly *Tuber magnatum* Pico, are one of the world's best-known and most-appreciated Italian foods. They generate a small but significant percentage of export value and attract many tourists, with beneficial effects for all the people living in truffle-producing areas. An awareness of these factors should push public authorities and businesses in the sector to launch practical initiatives to safeguard the fungi. Their scope should range from protecting truffle quality and consumer rights to preserving the environment where these remarkable but very fragile fruits of nature form and grow.
One clear example is the Alba white truffle quality certification scheme, created by the National Truffle Study Centre. It offers consumers a guarantee of the sensory quality of truffles that have been appraised by commissions of experts trained by the Centre. All truffle hunters and dealers in possession of particularly interesting truffles weighing more than 50 grams can request certification

from the desk present at fairs, where they will be given a seal that guarantees optimal quality.

A long-standing complaint is that during peak white truffle season, a number – some say most – of the truffles sold in Piedmont's markets and shops or served in its restaurants come from outside the region, or even outside Italy. Now, if these truffles are of the *Tuber magnatum* Pico species, we cannot say they are being "passed off as Alba white truffles". They are Alba white truffles, because that is the current and historically correct name for the most precious member of the *Tuber* genus. Naturally the truffle's geographic provenance should, according to current legislation, be indicated on the label. However, the reasons that make it preferable to buy a truffle from the Langhe instead of Istria when in Alba are the same as for any other local, "zero food miles" product: presumably great-

er freshness, greater traceability and the desire to leave the added value from the sale in the place where we live or are visiting.
Obviously, it is a different story when species other than *T. magnatum* Pico, of any provenance, are sold as Alba white truffles. The full extent of this type of fraud, punishable by law, is not known. However, given that in Italy all nine legally allowed species are commonly collected, it cannot be excluded that "minor" species are passed off as the more prized white and black truffles.

The *Tuber* species have significant differences between them, differences which are biological and morphological, not just sensory. The Alba white is fairly easy to identify, thanks mostly to its colour and seasonality. Distinguishing between the different black truffle varieties is harder. In an attempt to prevent fraud, public authorities and independent research institutes in the leading truffle-producing countries – Italy and France in particular – have been working for some time to develop scientifically valid systems for identifying species. In this regard, DNA analysis and mapping, already at an advanced stage for the black truffle, can be of great help.

Perhaps the most critical factor affecting the truffle world, however, is the deterioration of the conditions that guarantee the fungus's quantity and quality. That fewer and fewer truffles are being found has been observed for some time. Back in the 1930s, truffles were on the verge of finding perhaps not a "mass" market, but certainly one that

was greatly expanded compared to the elite gourmets of previous centuries. Even then, the fall in truffle production was being deplored. This decline was essentially due to destructive collecting systems and the uprooting of tall trees by landowners in reaction to damage caused by unskilled and greedy truffle hunters. Another phenomenon, cutting down wooded areas to plant vineyards, has increased greatly in the last 30 years, but mycologist Oreste Mattirolo was already blaming the vines in the 1920s. More generally, the arrival of "industrial" agriculture, mechanized and chemical based, has led to deep tilling of the land and the use of synthetic pesticides. The most fragile organisms, like symbiont fungi, are the first to be affected by the resulting environmental degradation. The depopulation and abandonment of marginal rural areas have also caused serious imbalances in the truffle environment, which will only be heightened by the hydrogeological and climatic changes facing us in the near future.
Remedying this situation as much as possible requires both legislative and programmatic interventions, with actions to increase the productivity of the truffle woodlands by restoring environmental conditions favourable to the development of truffles.

LAWS ON COLLECTING, CULTIVATING AND SELLING TRUFFLES

In Italy, the key reference for legislation about truffles is Law no. 752 of 16 December 1985, "Framework legislation regarding the collection, cultivation and selling of fresh or preserved truffles destined for consumption", which was slightly modified by Law no. 162 of 17 May 1991. These national regulations prohibit the sale and consumption of truffles from species other than the nine from the *Tuber* genus listed on page 11-12. Some regional laws make an exception for the sale of desert truffles (*Terfezia*, probably the genus that classical writers were referring to when they mentioned truffles), whose collection has a long tradition in certain areas like Puglia and Sardinia, particularly around Oristano.

By law, truffles can be freely gathered in woods and on uncultivated land, including pastures. In order to exercise their right of ownership over the fungi found in cultivated or controlled truffle woods (i.e. natural woodland improved by the planting of more truffle-producing trees), the leaseholder must mark the boundaries of the land with clearly visible notices reading *Raccolta di tartufi riservata* ("truffle collection reserved").

Truffle hunters must be aged over 14 and pass a suitability test. Regional authorities set their own regulations for the issuing of a non-transferrable permit to those who pass the test, which authorizes the holder to hunt and collect truffles anywhere in Italy. The permit may be subject to a fee, also set by the region. Truffles must be hunted with the help of a trained dog, and digging with a special truffle tool (a small hoe or spade) is only allowed in a spot where the dog has already started scratching.

Forbidden Activities

• continuous digging of the ground (in other words carried out with mechanical ploughs or scarifiers, which dig up to a depth of 80 centimetres to a metre) during the truffle season
• collecting unripe truffles
• not refilling holes after they have been dug to look for truffles
• hunting and collecting truffles from an hour after sunset until an hour before dawn, with some regional exceptions (adopted, for example, in Piedmont, where nocturnal hunting is allowed).

The law also sets the dates between which the different species can be collected, which can be varied regionally.

Rules for the Sale of Truffles Both Fresh...

Every form of sale of fresh truffles outside the collecting season is prohibited.

Fresh truffles must be displayed for sale separated by species and variety, fully mature and healthy, free of extraneous bodies and impurities. Whole truffles must be kept separate from broken ones. *Pezzi* ("pieces") are pieces of truffle with a diameter greater than half a centimetre and *tritume* ("shreds") are pieces with a diameter smaller than half a centimetre. They must also be sold separately, without any dirt or extraneous material, separated by species and variety.

Whether whole, in pieces or shreds, fresh truffles offered to the public for sale must be displayed with a printed card giving the Italian and Latin name of each species and variety and the geographic area where they were collected. The boundaries of these areas are established by the regional authorities after taking advice from the relevant provincial authorities.

... and Preserved

Preserved truffles are sold in hermetically sealed containers with labels giving the name and address of the packaging company, the name of the truffle in Latin and Italian, the classification and net weight of the drained truffles, as well as the indication *pelati* if the truffles have been peeled.

Preserved truffles are stored in water and salt or simply salt, with the option of adding wine, brandy or other spirits, which must be listed on the label. They must also be sterilized at around 120°C for the time required for the type of container.

The use of other substances (as long as they are not harmful to health) or a different preparation and preservation method must be indicated on the label using appropriate and easy-to-understand terms.

The use of colourings is not allowed.

The net weight indicated on the packaging must correspond to that of the drained truffles, with a maximum margin of 5%.

The contents of jars and bottles must have the following characteristics:

• transparent preserving or covering liquid, dark for *Tuber melanosporum*, *brumale* and *moschatum*, and yellowish of varying darkness for *T. magnatum*, *aestivum*, *uncinatum* and *mesentericum*

Enforcement and Sanctions

The Italian State Forestry Corps are responsible for enforcing the regulations. Provincial game wardens, the urban and rural police forces and volunteer guards appointed by cooperatives, consortia, organizations and associations for the protection of nature and the environment are also charged with enforcing the law.

For violations of the law, it is possible to pay a fine, within 60 days of the formal notification, of an amount equal to a third of the maximum possible fine.

Every violation of the regulations – in addition to obligatory denunciation to the judicial authorities depending on the circumstances – entails the confiscation of the product and is punished by administrative and monetary sanctions, as established by regional laws.

TARTUFO BIANCO
TUBER MAGNATUM PICO
TARTUFI EXTRA
Salsa al Tartufo del Piemonte

National Truffle Study Centre

The National Truffle Study Centre (*Centro Nazionale Studi Tartufo* in Italian) was established in 1996 as a branch of the Alba Bra Langhe Roero Tourism Board. It was presided over by Giacomo Oddero, who promoted the centre with the aim of improving knowledge about the truffle, a product with a strategic role to play in the development of food and wine tourism. Since 2000, the centre has been a legally autonomous association whose members include some of the main municipal administrations in the provinces of Alessandria, Asti and Cuneo. Its function is to bring together all of the key players in the truffle world, through the organizations that most represent them, to develop research, promotion and education policies. The Study Centre collaborates with Italy's most high-profile national research institutes, and since 2000 has been working in the field of sensory analysis, to define the aromatic profiles of the different species and to train qualified judges. Panels have been set up in Alba, Asti, Murisengo (Alessandria), Mondovì (Cuneo), Turin and San Giovanni d'Asso (Siena), where technical advice was also provided for the creation of a themed museum. Other groups represent the Truffle Towns, work in Istria, Croatia or evaluate products made with truffles.

The centre is strongly committed to protecting truffle-producing environments, increasingly threatened by human activity and the gradual abandonment of marginal areas. As well as studying the causes of the evident fall in truffle production, the centre is also experimenting with techniques for cultivating the land that could increase production. It is working with local authorities to develop a plan to safeguard truffle woodland environments, which will also be included in tourist itineraries.

Truffle Sensory Analysis

Smelling the precious Alba white truffle is easy – and enjoyable – enough, but classifying its most nuanced sensory characteristics is significantly harder. The Study Centre has been working on this project for years, with a huge sensory analysis programme which has led to the training of around a hundred qualified judges.
Tuber magnatum Pico is evaluated based on three of the five senses: sight, touch and smell.
The visual analysis involves an assessment of the integrity of the fruiting body. This is not a purely aesthetic factor, as a truffle in good condition will deteriorate much less quickly. The level of cleanliness is important as the presence of residual soil, as well as marring the appearance, can mask defects and imperfections. The visual analysis concludes with a valuation of the truffle's attractiveness, based on the personal perception of a specimen's

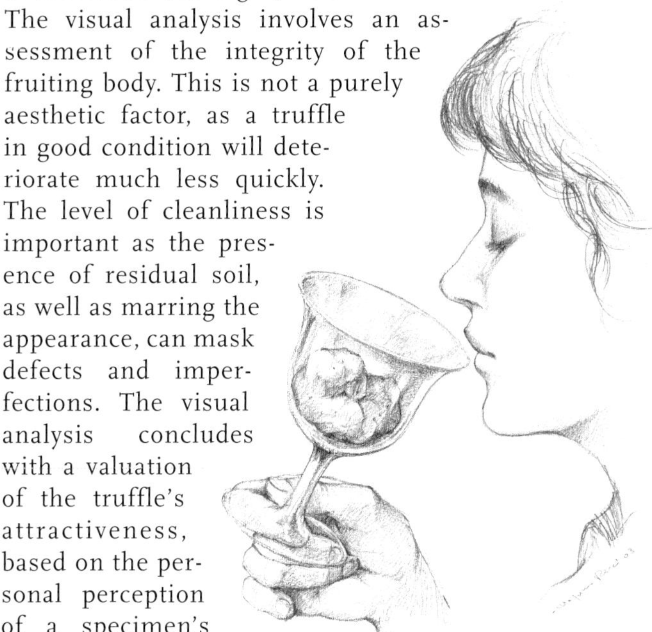

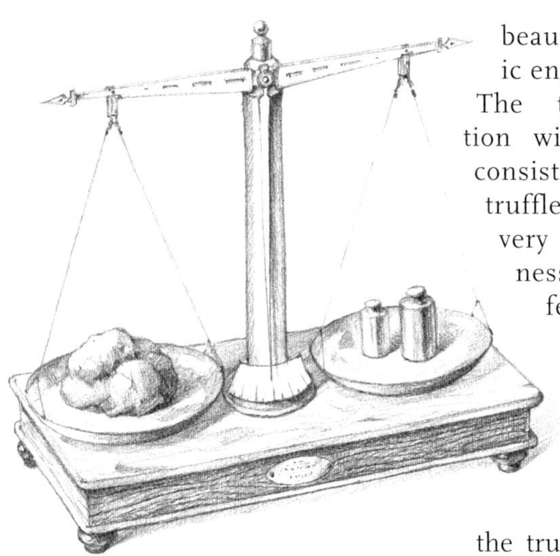

beauty and aesthetic enjoyability.

The tactile evaluation will analyse the consistency: a good truffle should have a very slight springiness and should feel turgid and compact, neither too hard nor with too much give.

The last step is smelling the truffle. The aroma is formed of a range of sensations, of varying intensity and breadth. It is this unique and appealing fragrance which has led to the truffle's supreme culinary success. The following descriptions can used to classify the aromatic composition of *Tuber magnatum*: fermented, mushroom, honey, hay, garlic, spices, wet earth, ammonia.

Reclaiming the Natural Truffle Woodlands

The Study Centre is working on studying and restoring the natural truffle woodlands that are suffering from dwindling production. The project involves agricultural works that re-establish the ecological order required for the natural growth of Alba white truffles.

The National Truffle Study Centre is based in Alba, Piazza Risorgimento 2. Tel. +39 0173 228190, e-mail info@tuber.it

✲ A Pact of Transparency: Truffle Club

The interesting Truffle Club initiative focuses on both protecting consumers and valuing the professionalism of those who use truffles every day throughout their season. The project was devised and is being run by the Institute for Wood Plants and the Environment (IPLA), a government-owned company whose majority stockholder is the Piedmont Regional Authority, and the National Truffle Study Centre.
Truffle Club is the largest Italian network of quality truffle-serving restaurants. Forging a pact of transparency with the consumer, restaurateurs who join the club undertake to respect the following code of ethics, committing:

• to only supply truffles of good quality (with an intense and enjoyable fragrance, sufficiently mature and in good condition)

• to clearly indicate on the menu the species being served (for example, *Tuber magnatum* Pico or Alba white truffle)

• to offer on the menu at least three or four dishes that can be paired with truffles

• to describe the dishes and the best truffle pairings to diners

• to list on the menu the names of the dishes in Italian with translations at least in English and ideally also in German

• to clearly display the price of the truffles

• to slice the truffle directly over the dish, in front of the client

• to not add natural-identical flavours to dishes featuring freshly sliced truffles

• to clearly and elegantly display some examples of truffles

• to respect the hunting season for *Tuber magnatum*, for example not serving white truffles before or after the dates set by regional law

• to allow diners to sample truffles not bought at the restaurant.

For more information about the project, visit the website www.truffleclub.org or send an email to info@truffleclub.org

Chapter 5

Buying Storing Using

del territorio

Where to Buy Truffles and How to Choose Them

The truffle is indisputably driving a flourishing economy – based on the sale of fresh and preserved fungi, but also the associated restaurant and tourism business – and yet defining its contours is practically impossible. The difficulties start with production estimates, due to the aura of mystery that envelops not only the truffle hunt but also the initial phases of truffle trading. Revealingly, the ISTAT[1] figures – released many years later – are always significantly lower than the probably more reliable data provided by those in the business. According to the owners of Urbani, based in Umbria and a national leader in the truffle trade, annual production is on average around 100 tonnes. From this discrepancy, we can deduce that the truffle market does not follow regular logic. Understandable, given that its focus is a rare, luxury, seasonal product, strongly influenced by weather patterns, sourced by a large group of professional and amateur hunters, supplied to restaurants and private consumers by the truffle hunters themselves or by various levels of intermediaries. Commercial operators, wholesalers and industrial processing companies make up a relatively small share of these middlemen.

Buying Fresh and Preserved Truffles

The aura of mystery extends from the hunt to the sale, but also to the consumption of truffles: a study carried out a few years ago for the University of Turin and the Piedmont Regional Authority[2] noted a similar "reticence" in the interviews with both hunters and the potential buyers visiting the fairs. The impression was of a not-very-transparent market, within which the shrewd consumer must be prudent, following a few simple tips.

The first is to look for fresh truffles not only, of course, during the harvest season (outside of which their sale is prohibited), but also in their places of origin and from retailers who belong or at least are connected to the associations of hunters. In general, purchases at fairs offer a good guarantee. Here, consumers can easily compare different prices and qualities, and the infiltration of illegal truffle hunters is unlikely. Exhibitions, markets and, more generally, specialized fairs often include specific opportunities for consumers to inform and educate themselves. They can be useful

for learning how to tell one species from another, how to check the ripeness of a truffle and how to recognize the merits and defects of the specimens on sale.
As for preserved truffles, processing methods in Italy were established by the 1985 framework law and must be specified on the label. Not many companies work in this field, and their prominence serves as a guarantee in and of itself. Our reservations come from the objective limitations of the ambition to "can" the fragrance of the truffle, particularly the incomparable white truffle. The development in recent years of new preserving techniques (cold and vacuum extraction of the moisture, producing dehydrated truffles; a patented project for extracting the truffle's natural aroma in the form of an essential oil) has inspired considerable and well-founded interest. However, the sensory yield of products preserved using the methods set out in the 1985 law continues to be modest, and certainly does not justify their prices. Not to mention that we should be asking a basic question: does it make sense to lavish so much money and energy on realizing the dream of having the most prized of truffles available year-round? Why try to "deseasonalize" a product whose limited availability (in terms of season and quantity) is one of the most fascinating things about it? If we could, in theory, enjoy white truffles 365 days out of 365, instead of waiting for them to ripen according to the rhythms of nature, wouldn't their consumption become boring?

Truffle Flavour

The so-called truffle-flavoured products require a certain caution: oils, butter, sauces, cheeses, pâtés, flours, rice, tagliatelle, filled pastas, even sweets and whatever else it occurs to people to flavour with truffle. To compensate for the alteration of flavour and fragrance caused by the processing methods used for these industrial products, synthetic "truf-

fle flavour" is added. This substance has nothing to do with the actual fungus, except for a chemical equivalence to its main aromatic component. Many truffle-flavoured products on the market contain this substance – legal and harmless, but definitely lacking the aromatic complexity of a fresh Alba white truffle. Of course, those who think they cannot afford to buy a fresh truffle, or a shower of shavings over a plate of tagliatelle in a restaurant, might be happy to take home a little bottle of truffle oil as a souvenir. But, in the best of all possible worlds that we can imagine, truffles – particularly white truffles – should be eaten fresh, in the ways codified by regional tradition or inspired by the chef's creativity.

1. Italy's National Institute of Statistics, a public research organization which carries out censuses, family surveys and economic studies on prices, businesses, trade, employment, etc

2. Livia Maistrelli, Angela Mosso, *Il settore tartuficolo piemontese: analisi economica delle tartufaie coltivate e approfondimenti sul mercato dei tartufi e dei prodotti derivati*, Department of Agricultural Economics and Engineering at the University of Turin and the Mountain and Forest Economics Office of the Piedmont Regional Authority, Turin 2006.

What Is a Truffle Made Of?

A fresh truffle is made up of over 80% water. The average chemical composition of a *Tuber magnatum* and a *T. melanosporum* weighing 100 grams is as follows:

Water	82.58-82.80
Ash	1.97-1.70
Total nitrogen	0.88-0.87
Non-protein nitrogen	0.23-0.14
Protein	4.13-4.50
Lipids	2.08-1.90
Soluble carbohydrates	0.36-0.17
Dietary fibre	8.43-8.13

Also present are infinitesimal quantities of minerals (potassium, calcium, sodium, magnesium, phosphorous, iron, zinc, copper) and vitamins (B1, B2, B3, C). The truffle's value, therefore, does not come from its nutritional benefits, which are practically zero, but its ability to bring pleasure to the eater. This characteristic is responsible for the huge difference in market price between species with almost identical chemical compositions.

For more information on white truffle prices, you can refer to the *Borsa Nazionale del Tartufo*, a kind of price index started in 1996 by the Asti Chamber of Commerce (www.at.camcom.gov.it), while the retail prices of the four main types of truffle (*T. magnatum*, *T. melanosporum*, bianchetto and scorzone) charged by Acqualagna's dealers are provided daily at http://acqualagna.com/fiere-tartufo/fiera-nazionale. A weekly updated price guide can also be found on www.tuber.it

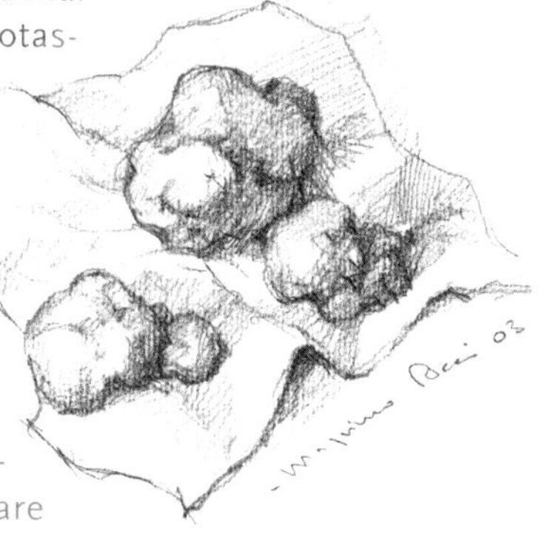

Storing and Cleaning Truffles at Home

"How do you store truffles?" we once asked a restaurateur friend. "In your memory", came the laconic response, followed nonetheless by a series of suggestions in line with the advice from experts, which we will shortly provide. But that apparently paradoxical quip contained a profound truth. Their short life, the impossibility of prolonging their fragrance and flavour for more than a few days, the memory of the pleasure brought by the last taste, the anxious wait for the next season: all these factors contribute to the value of these "diamonds of the kitchen".

So how do we store truffles? Once we acknowledge that, like all fresh foods, they are best consumed immediately after harvesting, or at least within a couple of days, certain methods are suitable for the short-term storage (no longer than a week) of all types of truffle:

- they must be kept chilled, though at a temperature that is not too low (the ideal is between 3° and 6°C), so as to slow decomposition.
- after wrapping them in a cloth or layers of slightly dampened paper towels, they should be refrigerated. However, different schools of thought exist as to what they should be stored in. Most experts suggest placing them in a closed container – ideally made of glass – so as to isolate the truffles from possible contamination and reduce the dispersal of their fragrance, as well as safeguarding other foods in the refrigerator. Others claim that as living organisms, truffles suffer from impris-

onment. They limit themselves to wrapping them further in three or four layers of paper towels, and resign themselves to having other foods be "infected" by the truffle's overwhelming, penetrating aroma.

• others advise vacuum packing, in which case the truffle can be stored in an optimal condition for up to ten days rather than just a week.

There are no other systems suitable for white truffles, while for black truffles, which tend to be cooked, there are a few more options. For example, after careful cleaning and thorough drying, they can be grated and mixed with top-quality butter melted over a bain-marie, then stored in tightly sealed jars. This paste can be used for many purposes for a fairly long time. Storage in extra-virgin olive oil, which would in any case be short-lived, is inadvisable. The truffle's deterioration is slowed, but the oil will spoil and you can end up with a rancidity that means neither ingredient can be used. It might be traditional in many Italian regions, but the habit of placing a truffle in a jar of uncooked rice is also out, as the rice's dehydrating properties will dry out the truffle.

Lastly, the authors of a book on the Piedmontese black truffle (Elio Archimede et al, *L'altro tartufo del Piemonte*, Sagittario, Agliano Terme 2010) recall "an ancient method used in France, particularly Provence" for storing truffes du Périgord, which is also used in Italy, at least in the area around Monferrato. The truffles are placed in dark glass or terracotta jars, with salt. The well-sealed containers are sterilized at 110°C for a couple of hours, then cooled in woollen cloths and stored in a cellar. "The Provençals claim that this system allows the black truffles to be stored for a very long time, for years even."

When it comes to cleaning, for both black and white truffles a fairly stiff brush, a paintbrush and a damp cloth should be used to remove the dirt that is most likely present, particularly in the cracks and folds of the peridium. Additionally, any spots with traces of rot or insect attacks should be removed with a small knife. If necessary, white truffles can be washed with cold water before use, brushed and then left to sit for at least 10 minutes. After being cleaned, and just before cooking, the black truffle can be rinsed under cold or warm running water, then dried thoroughly. "It will make it easier if we want to slice it, but most importantly we will avoid any water coming into contact with the gleba (the internal part), which will diminish its fragrance."

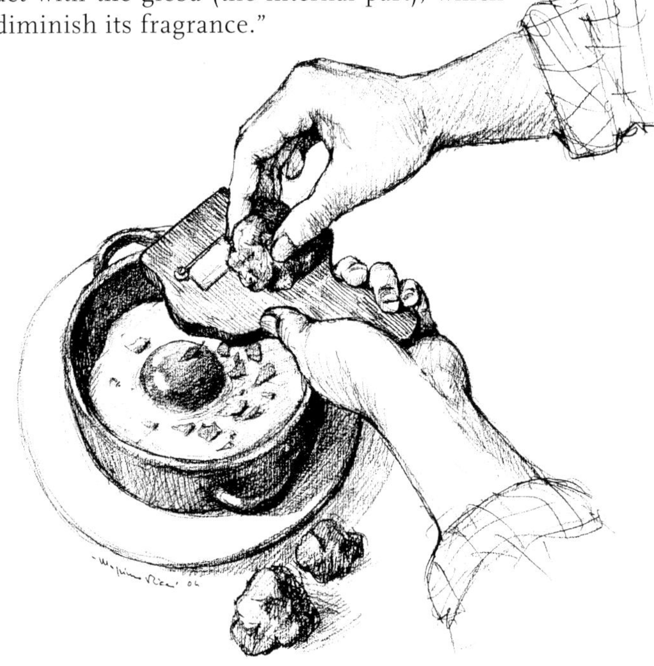

THE ALBA WHITE TRUFFLE MYTHS AND TRUTHS

The National Truffle Study Centre has published a "quality charter" for the white truffle, a kind of pocket guide for consumers, helpful when choosing which truffle to buy, identifying the most common defects and sorting out the facts from the legends that have been associated with the *Tuber* family for millennia.

False theories about truffles

In the past, the truffle was believed to be...

- witches' food
- an animal
- a mineral

Today, some people still think the truffle is...

- a tuber
- a parasitic fungus
- a disease of the soil
- a potato

In fact, it is an underground symbiotic fungus

If a white truffle costs...
a little: take care
a lot: some myths are based on truth
too much: unique experiences have a price

Morphological characteristics

Smooth peridium, at times cracked, pale yellow tending towards grey in mediocre specimens.
Spherical or slightly flattened shape, with protuberances caused by the soil type.
Compact gleba, brownish in colour, becoming darker as it ripens, run through by whitish veins made up of filaments of hyphae.

Sensory characteristics

Once fully ripe, it gives off an intense fragrance, composed of aromas that recall garlic, hay, wet earth, honey, mushrooms and spices.
The flavour is very pleasant.

Environmental Conditions

Truffles develop in cool, damp conditions, around 10-15 centimetres below the ground, at an average temperature of 6°C.
As the spores spread, a mycelium develops, which wraps around the root tips of specific tree species (English oak, Turkey oak, sessile oak, downy oak, black poplar, silver poplar, goat willow, white willow, linden, hop hornbeam, hazel).

The Soil

Clayey-chalky, moist, with a neutral pH, low in organic material, nitrogen and phosphorous and rich in potassium.

Collecting Truffles

Truffles are collected in the autumn, within a season set by the regional authority. Truffle hunting is allowed in woods and on uncultivated land, but is banned in private truffle woodlands and areas reforested within the last 15 years.

Tips for Buying

Consult reliable sources on the market trends.
Check that the species is correct.
Check that the holes and cracks are not filled with soil.
Check that the truffle has not been dusted with cornmeal to change the colour.
Check that the smell is pleasant all over.
Check the level of maturity.
Check the cleanliness.
Check that the truffle has not been reconstituted.

Storage

Somewhere cool with a temperature between 3° and 6°C, ideally wrapped in paper towels and stored in a glass container. In this way, a fresh truffle can be preserved for around a week. Poor storage can accelerate the deterioration process.

Possible Defects

Not ripe enough. When the truffle is not fully mature, its characteristics make it unsuitable for consumption.
Unpleasant smells. Sometimes a deteriorating truffle can give off odours of ammonia, methane and fermentation.
Presence of mycosis. This causes brown spots to devel-

op on the peridium, which can change the fragrance and texture, altering enjoyability.
Lack of integrity. Certain kinds of deterioration can be caused by parasites, or the truffle-hunting dog might have left scratches from its claws.
Rubberiness. This characteristic is found in older specimens or those not stored properly.

Consumption

White truffles should ideally be served uncooked, as a seasoning, shaved into thin slivers over simple and fairly bland dishes.

The Alba white truffle

IS HUNTED...	WITH PIGS	IT IS VERY HARD TO TRAIN A PIG
	ONLY AT NIGHT	WHY ON EARTH?
IS FOUND...	YEAR-ROUND	FROM SEPTEMBER TO JANUARY
IS STORED...	IN RISE	WRAPPED IN PAPER TOWELS
	FOR MONTHS	FOR NO MORE THAN 10 DAYS
	IN THE FREEZER	LOSE ITS FLAVOUR AND FRAGRANCE
	IN OIL	FERMENT
	IN BRINE	LOSE ALL OF ITS CHARACTERISTICS
IN THE KITCHEN...	IT IS PEELED	IT SHOULD BE CLEANED WELL, BUT NOT PEELED
	IT IS EATEN WHOLE	IT IS SLICED INTO THIN SHAVINGS
	IT IS EATEN CHOPPED	IT IS SLICED INTO THIN SHAVINGS
	IT IS GRATED	PLEASE SLICE IT INTO THIN SHAVINGS
	IT IS COOKED	NEVER!
IT CAN GROW...	CULTIVATED	UNFORTUNATELY IT ONLY GROWS WILD
	IN ALL KINDS OF SOIL	ONLY IN CERTAIN SPECIFIC ENVIRONMENTS
	IN SYMBIOSIS WITH ANY PLANT	ONLY WITH A FEW SPECIES

Black and White Truffles in the Kitchen and at the Table

In Italy, *Tuber melanosporum* Vitt. features in the gastronomic traditions of the peninsula's central regions. The black truffle is suited to cooking, because its flavour can be perceived better with fat and after heating. However, it can also be eaten raw; a versatile product, it is suited to various culinary uses. Depending on local custom, the black truffle can be found in starters, first courses and mains, in various forms: minced and mixed with mushrooms and extra-virgin olive oil to top warm crostini, ground in a mortar with oil and salt to make a flavourful sauce for pasta, sliced and cooked together with roast meats or mixed with other ingredients in fillings and stuffings. The black truffle is particularly popular in France, where it has been heavily cultivated, with excellent results, since the 19th century (almost all the *truffes du Périgord* that pour onto the French market come from cultivated truffle orchards). The truffle features in many dishes: finely chopped on top of eggs *à la coque* or *poché*; sliced over crostini, potatoes or other vegetables like carrots, artichokes and celery, or used in other French or international gastronomic specialties.

Tuber magnatum Pico is eaten almost exclusively raw: the only exception, reported by the late Marco Guarnaschelli Gotti (in *Grande Enciclopedia Illustrata della Gastronomia*, selection from Reader's Digest, Milan 1990-Mondadori, Milan 2007), is the *tegamino alla lodigiana* (or *alla parmigiana*, depending on whether the cheese used is Grana Lodigiano or Parmigiano Reggiano). "Now fallen out of use due to the cost," he recounts, it involves baking truffles in the oven. The dish "is originally from the area

around the Po between Pavia and Piacenza and dates back to when the Oltrepo Pavese and Piacentino hills abundantly supplied this area with white truffles of excellent quality. Unlike today, they were not sold on the national market and therefore were available relatively cheaply. The most traditional cheese would be the rare Grana Lodigiano."

Apart from this isolated example, the advice (and sometimes the distraught plea) of gastronomes and gastrophiles is enjoy the white truffle uncooked, shaved into thin slivers with a special gadget and scattered over fairly neutral dishes whose delicate flavour allows the truffle to best express its complex, intense and overwhelming aroma. The standard dose is 10 grams, but if the truffle is at just the right ripeness, 7 or 8 might be enough. Eggs cooked in butter, raw veal, *fonduta* (Italian fondue), *tajarin* (thin egg pasta) and a plain risotto are the traditional Piedmontese dishes best suited to showcasing the endowments of these "diamonds of the kitchen". We offer them here, along with seven more creative recipes developed by chefs from renowned restaurants in the Langhe and Roero. The truffle is an ancient but not old-fashioned product, faithful to tradition without being embalmed in it, for all lovers of good food, not just elite circles. The measure of the truffle's ability to adapt to innovation is clear from the dishes that chefs have developed to meet the expectations of gourmets of all generations, with respect for its history and subtle creativity.

Beyond the White Truffle

"... it would be good to start to appreciate other species of truffles as well. Used in the right way, they prove to have sensory qualities so far unknown to the majority of consumers. There are truffles which can be found cheaply throughout the year, which can be used to flavour our foods with good results. On this subject, remember that black truffles (*Tuber melanosporum* Vittadini) can be used until March. From April to May, the bianchetto (*Tuber borchii*) can be used in soups, as it adds character to broths. From July we find the scorzone or black summer truffle (*Tuber aestivum* Vittadini) and, in late autumn, *Tuber uncinatum* Chatin, which are both excellent on salads, in fillings and in sauces. In August and September we have *Tuber macrosporum* Vittadini, an excellent black truffle with a white-truffle fragrance, though it is best not to exaggerate with quantities because it has a very strong aroma and can prove to be a little indigestible. The season for the white truffle (*Tuber magnatum* Pico), the undisputed king of the table, runs from September to December. Finally, the winter offers not only the already mentioned black truffle, but also the black winter truffle (*Tuber brumale* Vittadini) which costs much less (a third of the black) and is excellent for flavouring salads, risottos and other dishes."

Enrico Vigna, *Trifolau e tartufi. Aspetti antropologici dell'economia rurale tra Langhe e Monferrato*, Province of Asti-Brigati, Genoa 1999

Short and Long Itineraries for a "Slow" Tourism

Piedmont
Langhe, Roero and Monferrato

☞ Every year, around 300,000 tourists stay overnight in Alba, Bra and the Langhe and Roero in general. Almost two-thirds come from outside Italy, from dozens of countries on all continents. They come from the end of winter to the late autumn, for stays that generally brief, but not too brief (the average visit is almost three nights, many in holiday farms and B&Bs). As we can presume that for every "stationary" tourist at least two make a day trip to the area, it is possible to estimate visitor numbers of close to a million a year.

Within the Langhe and Roero district (made up of 94 municipalities on either side of the River Tanaro, including the administrative centres of Alba and Bra), the statistics show figures that go sharply against the trend of general crisis, and for years they have been on the increase. These are the after-effects of long-term investment focused on food and wine, on the pioneering promotion of truffles, wines and the typical dishes of the southern Piedmontese hills. It is the result of a "legendary commercial entrepreneurialism which has been able to turn the hostile hills of *La Malora** into a paradise for gourmets" (*Vivermeglio*, Cuneo-based monthly magazine, February 2007).

But the tourists from all over the world who visit this land, blessed by nature and made welcoming by human effort, do not ask only for excellent meals in refined restaurants or rustic osterias, visits to prestigious wineries and specialty shops stocked with excellent foods. They also ask (and they will ask more and more, following the inclusion of the Langhe, Roero and Monferrato vineyard landscape in the list of UNESCO's protected World Heritage sites) for tranquillity, respect for the environment, visitable historic buildings, open and functioning museums and other cultural centres, excursions to places where the presence

of humans has harmoniously blended with the natural setting and a sincere and warm relationship with the local people. To these guests, not necessarily rich but definitely cultured, sociable and curious, who know many things but want to learn more and who consider every journey as a way of doing just that, we suggest six itineraries for discovering the truffle hills. They can be followed using "slow" tourism methods (on foot, by bike, on horseback), or, with slight modifications, by car or motorbike or – armed with the patience of a saint – by public transport.

On this subject, we should remind you that the majority of the 94 towns within the Alba-Bra tourism district are currently connected to each other and the rest of the world by road alone. The only rail line that seems to be (relatively) safe from drastic cuts is the section of the Cavallermaggiore-Asti line linking Alba and Bra. Otherwise, the regional passenger service is suspended on both the Castagnole delle Lanze-Asti stretch and, for some time now, the Asti-Mortara. This hampers a direct rail connection with Milan, which would offer an alternative to changing in Turin and would be of strategic importance in light of Expo 2015. Meanwhile, the Bra-Ceva line

has been abandoned for almost 20 years by now, ever since the 1994 flood, to the detriment of relationships between the towns of the Langhe and the west of Liguria.

It is worth reflecting on the potential advantages of a restoration of the tracks, based on experiences with tourist trains around Europe. These lines, ideally flanked by cycle paths, could once again connect the truffle district with the Ligurian Riviera and the Po Valley megalopolis, rendering accessible in an environmentally friendly way what is known as "the quadrilateral of taste" marked out by the railway lines between Bra, Cherasco, Monchiero-Dogliani, Carrù, Bastia Mondovì, Mondovì, San Giuseppe di Cairo, Acqui Terme, Nizza (Asti), Canelli, Santo Stefano Belbo, Castagnole delle Lanze and Alba.

The six itineraries, all starting from the Langhe's capital and home of the Truffle Fair, have as their (at least symbolic) destination the truffle woodlands restored by the National Truffle Study Centre in Barbaresco, Rocca d'Arazzo (Asti), Montà, Monchiero, Murazzano and Priero. This last village is reached by passing through Vezza d'Alba, home to an educational truffle wood, and the plan is to open an Alba White Truffle Museum here, on the initiative of a foundation made up of representatives from the City of Alba, the Roero Hill Community, the Montà municipality, the International Alba White Truffle Fair Organizing Committee, the Alba Bra Langhe Roero Tourism Board and the Montà RoeroAttiva Foundation Committee. The museum will be a highly innovative multimedia structure, designed to protect and promote a cultural heritage that has characterized southern Piedmont for centuries.

Even the smallest villages cited in the itineraries, or reachable by a small deviation from the main route, have a range of accommodation options that offer a good level of comfort, in settings that are almost always relaxing and rural. Most importantly, there is not an urban neighbourhood, secluded village or tiny countryside hamlet without at least one restaurant – Michelin-starred or rustically casual – where diners can sample the cuisine unanimously acclaimed as one of the best and most characteristic in the world.

On the subject of the past and present role of restaurants in the truffle district's success with tourists, we thought it might be interesting to publish some thoughts from a non-Piedmontese visitor to the Langhe, who writes: "Why, when talking about white truffles, is Alba the first name out of everyone's mouth? Why Alba, and not other areas, where truffles are probably more abundant and of similar quality? 'They started first' some will say. Others believe that the Langhe's dealers and restaurateurs only buy the finest truffles from around Italy, and with these they uphold the name of Alba in the world. Some claim that the Langhe are lucky to be home to a wine-producing area of global interest, with thousands of tourists who supplement their enological visit with a purchase of truffles or a truffled dish in a restaurant. Who is right? Everyone. Much of the credit however must go to the Langhe's restaurateurs, who always rise to the occasion. I've eaten many times in restaurants in those parts and I have never been served a dish in which a different variety has been disguised as a white truffle using the usual chemical extract tricks, even in the humblest of premises. I have sampled excellent white truffle dishes and equally excellent dishes with scorzone truffles. In this way, the consumer can develop a culture of recognizing the flavours, without being taken for a ride, and can begin to understand the seasonal nature of truffles and the difference in costs between a white truffle dish and a black truffle dish. These are the truffle basics. Alba is Alba not because the best truffles are found there, but because in Alba

the best truffles are bought and used. The gastronomic offerings are numerous and excellent, and everyone wants to develop and give their best – not to become rich quickly. That will come later, in time."

We suggest you also take your time with the itineraries we describe below, travelling slowly and with curiosity. Happy travels, and buon appetito.

* Beppe Fenoglio's novel *La Malora* (*Ruin*) was responsible for perpetuating an image of the Langhe before the war as poverty-stricken and derelict.

Alba-Barbaresco-Neive-Alba

One Emperor, Seven Brothers Four Great Wines

This route is fairly short, less than 10 kilometres, but we will extend it a bit to visit two other villages within the small Barbaresco DOCG zone, Treiso and Neive. We're on the right bank of the River Tanaro, which has run at the foot of these hills, carving out impressive ravines, for the last 100,000 years. Previously, the river headed north after reaching the confluence with the Stura di Demonte downstream from Ceva, flowing into the Po between what are now Carignano and Carmagnola. One of the six sub-areas recognized by UNESCO as a World Heritage site, the land here is densely planted with vines. Moscato, dolcetto and barbera grapes are grown in addition to nebbiolo, and once made into wine can use the denominations Moscato d'Asti, Dolcetto d'Alba and Barbera d'Alba.

Leave the city from Piazza Monsignor Grassi, taking Viale Cherasca, crossing the bridge over the stream of the same name and climbing up to Altavilla, a pleasant spot in the hilly outskirts of Alba. From the top of the rise, we then descend again to the plain of the Seno d'Elvio. The watery guiding thread of this itinerary, the stream

lends its name to the first stop on our route. San Rocco Seno d'Elvio is a pretty little village with a handful of houses, some of which falls within the DOCG area. The oldest bottle yet found to bear the (handwritten) label "Barbaresco", dating from 1877, is stored here in the Cascine Drago cellars. But the wine then was very different from how it is now. The first experiments with Barbaresco were made in Neive in the 1860s by the French merchant and enologist Louis Oudart, then continued 30 years later in the Barbaresco castle by ampelographer Domizio Cavazza, founder and director of Alba's Enological School. Going much further back in history, nearby Pertinace was probably the birthplace of the Roman emperor Publius Helvius Pertinax, Commodus's successor, born in 126 AD. Like Commodus, he was

also assassinated, killed by the Praetorians barely three months into his reign.

We are now within the boundaries of the municipality of Treiso, formed fairly recently, in 1957, after detaching itself from Barbaresco. The village's little square is an extraordinary balcony looking out over the vine-covered hills of the Langhe, the other side of the Tanaro and the curve of the Alps, a panorama that led a character in one of Beppe Fenoglio's stories to say: "This world is made for living in peace." A short walk leads to a different but equally impressive view, over the gorge of the Rocche dei Sette Fratelli, the "rocks of the seven brothers", the setting for many legends that live on in the collective memory. This geological formation is caused by the erosion common to the marly heights of the Roero and this part of the Langhe.

Spectacular gullies also characterize the Barbaresco slope facing the Tanaro, topped by the 11th-century tower, seemingly hanging in the void. It is the symbol of the village, which is just over 5 kilometres from Treiso. We are in what the Romans called *Barbarica silva,* inhabited by the Ligurian Statielli tribe. The Romans colonized the area with a settlement known as *Villa Martis.* The current village was fortified in the Middle Ages and a grouping of protected houses developed around an older castle, not the current 18th-century building, the former residence of the Galleani counts. The site of the first Barbaresco cooperative winegrowers' association, founded in 1894 by the aforementioned Domizio Cavazza, today it is a prestigious winery. Since 1986, the nearby former church of San Donato has housed the Barbaresco Regional Enoteca, showcasing over 250 labels from 130 local winemakers.

Another 5 kilometres and we reach Neive, whose historic old centre – named one of Italy's most beautiful villages – has preserved its medieval layout, with winding cobbled lanes, a 13th-century clock tower and elegant buildings. In the cellars of the town hall, the Bottega dei Quattro Vini celebrates Neive's four enological glories: Barbaresco, Barbera, Dolcetto and Moscato. But the village's alcoholic attractions extend beyond wine; "angelic" Romano Levi has been making exceptional grappa here for decades, while in the hamlet of Bricco a microbrewery produces excellent top-fermented beers.

Alba-Mango-Santo Stefano Belbo Canelli-Nizza Monferrato-Asti-Alba

Moscato, Barbera and Great Literature

This itinerary reconnects with the previous one, because from Neive, travelling just over 5 kilometres along a winding road that climbs through vineyards alternated with hazelnuts and broadleaved woods, you will reach the ridge between the Tinella and Belbo valleys. Here, at over 520 metres above sea level, is Mango. Probably based on the remains of a Roman colony, it was an important stopping point along the "salt routes" between Piedmont and Liguria. The village was founded in the early Middle Ages by Asti as an outpost against its eternal enemy Alba, uniting the inhabitants of four pre-existing settlements. The current castle, built in the 17th century by the marquesses of Busca on the ruins of a 13th-century fortress, is home to a restaurant and the Regional Enoteca of the Moscato Hills.

We are indeed inside the production zone for the Asti DOCG for this celebrated white wine, which covers about 50 municipalities in southern Piedmont. The sparkling version is synonymous around the world with festive toasts, and even Ernest Hemingway testified to its international and long-standing fame in the second chapter of *A Farewell to Arms* (Scribner's, New York 1929). In the late autumn of 1916, in Gorizia, behind the Italo-Austrian front on the Isonzo, Lieutenant Frederic Henry watches the snow fall "looking out of the window of the bawdy house, the house for officers, where I sat with a friend and two glasses drinking a bottle of Asti", a phrase that seems to imply an appreciation denied other Piedmontese wines. The following summer, sitting in Milan's Galleria with Catherine Barkley, the novel's protagonist prefers "dry white capri iced in a bucket." In the collective imagination, Asti is primarily a sparkling wine, but a natural Moscato also exists, mentioned in the most celebrated of poems by Guido Gozzano (Turin, 1883-1916): " 'Would you care for some muscatel?' – 'That would be a most welcome libation.' / And so with a calm smile they sat themselves down for some good conversation." ("Grandmother Speranza's Friend" in *The Man I Pretend to Be*, translated by Michael Palma, Princeton University Press, Princeton 1981).

Near Mango, an open-air museum links some of the most significant locations connected to writer Beppe Fenoglio, including, in the Castino area in the hills opposite, San Bovo, with the "Johnny the Partisan path" and Pavaglione, the farmhouse where much of *La Malora* (*Ruin*) is set. Also worth visiting in Mango is the hamlet of San Donato, reachable via a pleasant walk through the woods, a rebel stronghold during the Resistance and a collection point for the war supplies airdropped by the Allies. In the middle of the village, the former primary school is now a "Memory House", furnished with objects and images from the past by the cultural association Arvangia ("revenge").

Literary references abound in the brief stretch of road that leads to Santo Stefano, the easternmost municipality in the province of Cuneo and the main hub for the middle Belbo Valley, known for its significant wine production (almost entirely dedicated to Asti Spumante) and perhaps even more for being the birthplace of one of the great 20th-century Italian writers. Cesare Pavese was born here on 9 September, 1908, somewhat by chance, given that his parents, resident in Turin, had only come to Santo Stefano for the summer holidays. Due to various tragic family circumstances, Pavese spent his early childhood in the town. He later returned on various occasions, and throughout his life the place remained vivid in his memory and imagination. *La luna e i falò* (*The Moon and the Bonfires*), written a few months before his suicide on 27 August, 1950, is the novel that best exemplifies the relationship with the Belbo hills that for Pavese were "the gates of the world". A piece of his heart remained here even after moving to Turin for his studies – his encounter with the teacher Augusto Monti, a great educator and writer from Monastero Bormida, was to prove very influential – falling in love with the American narrative, being arrested and imprisoned in Calabria for anti-fascism, the collections of poems, the novels and stories, the essays, the diaries, the correspondence with the intellectuals of the time and the meticulous work of translation and editing for Giulio Einaudi's publishing company.

Since 2004, the Cesare Pavese Foundation, which took over the research activities of the Cesare Pavese Study Centre, founded in 1973, has been working to raise the profile of the writer and his work. Based in the 14th-century Santi Giacomo e Cristoforo confraternity, a well-stocked library and various temporary initiatives welcome scholars and enthusiasts from around the world. A Pavese pilgrimage would also have to include Pavese's birthplace, along the road to Canelli, and the sawmill of his close friend Pinolo Scaglione, Nuto in *The Moon and the Bonfires*. Santo Stefano Belbo is one of the few towns where pallone elastico, a typically Langhe sport (just as tamburello is typical of the Monferrato), continues to be played competitively on a well-preserved court. The continuation of the tradition was certainly given a boost by the fact that Augusto Manzo (1911-1982), the greatest *balón* champion of all time, winner of ten national shields, eight for palla a pugno and two for pallone col bracciale, was born in Santo Stefano.

The next stop along our itinerary is Canelli, just outside the province of Cuneo, 157 metres above sea level with a population of 10,770, considered the modern capital of Asti Spumante. This role is confirmed by its high number of large wineries and inclusion among the "core zones" of the UNESCO project to protect the Piedmontese vineyard landscape. The success of the landscape's nomination as a World Heritage site was due in no small part to a unique feature in Canelli: the system of monumental tunnels where the bottles produced in the town have been stored since at least the 19th century. Some of these "underground wine cathedrals" are open to the public, starting from the castle's cellars. Now an elegant villa owned by a winemaking family, the castle, which dominates the town, has a 17th-century layout but was rebuilt in the last century.

If you happen to be around here on the third weekend in June, you can witness a magnificent and exciting historical re-enactment, with thousands of costumed characters portraying an event from 1613: the heroic actions and resounding victory of the Canellesi while besieged by the troops of Carlo I of Gonzaga-Nevers, Duke of Mantua and the Monferrato.

The hairpin bends of the road that lead south, towards Cassinasco and Bubbio in the Bormida Valley, offer sweeping views over the moscato vineyards. However, we will head in the opposite direction, following the River Belbo's route via footpaths or the main road, to reach Nizza

Monferrato, an important agricultural and commercial hub. One of the centres for Moscato production, it also falls within the Barbera del Monferrato DOCG zone, and has given its name to a Superiore version of Barbera d'Asti DOCG. On a par with Barbera d'Alba, these wines make the most of the red grape perhaps most characteristic of Piedmont, celebrated in the Regional Enoteca in Palazzo Crova di Vaglio, also the location of a Museum of Taste. Nizza's gastronomic merits do not end with its great wines. It is also home to at least one excellent vegetable variety, the *cardo gobbo* or hunchbacked cardoon, grown in the sandy soils along the Belbo River using an ancient whitening technique. The only cardoon eaten raw, it is an irreplaceable element in the entourage of vegetables served alongside the garlic-and-anchovy dip *bagna caoda*. But the little town is also proud to be the birthplace of Francesco Cirio (1836-1900), a self-made man and pioneer in the food preservation industry.

From Nizza we need to reach Asti via minor roads, even if travelling by car, so as to pass by the Rocca d'Arazzo truffle wood. This village of 950 inhabitants on the right bank of the Tanaro has been the subject of a thousand disputes; initially it belonged to the bishop of Asti, then in 1198 it passed to the city of Asti, only to return to the Church in 1221. Thirty years later it was enfeoffed to Druino de Cacherano; in 1379 it passed to Gian Galeazzo Visconti, the lord of Milan, then in 1499 to Louis XII of France, in 1526 to Emperor Charles V and finally, in 1705, to the House of Savoy. Reconstructing the identities of the feudal lords in the area helps to understand the reasons for the immense prestige enjoyed during the two and half centuries (1095-1342) of the Republic of Asti, at the time one of the most important political and economic entities in north-western Italy.

The Cacheranos were a family from Asti who had acquired nobility and power by providing money-changing services and loans on pledge in their hometown but also in Genoa and on the other side of the Alps, from Burgundy to Breisgau, Savoy to Flanders. Much of the free city's ruling class was involved in similar businesses, encouraged in 1141 by the imperial authorization to mint coins and in 1225 by the privileges granted by the King of France, used by the "Lombards" (as Asti's merchant-bankers were known) to avoid the canonical accusation of usury. Despite threats of excommunication, it seems that in the 14th century the average interest rate was over 40%. The resulting profits were invested into agricultural estates and castles, and later in the acquisition of seigniorial rights, and led to significant economic development and a huge expansion of the territory controlled by he city. This prosperity, and Asti's republican independence, were brought to an end by the perennial conflict between Guelphs and Ghibellines. Eventually a bloody civil war at the end of the 13th century, lasting almost half a century, resulted in subjection to Robert of Anjou, a representative of the dynasty previously most troubled by the Astigiano government.

The city of today has an important wine and white truffle trade and preserves significant traces of its glorious past. The urban layout is still based on the decumanus of the Roman *Hasta*. This main east-west axis is named, like the main piazza, after the city's most illustrious son, dramatist and poet Vittorio Alfieri (1749-1803). The architecture includes Gothic religious masterpieces but also tower-houses and palaces belonging to notables from the old Republic. The Guelph families included the Solaris, the Fallettis, the Malabailas and the Trojas, while the Ghibellines included the Guttuaris, the Isnardis, the Scarampis, the Alfieris, the De Castellos and the Turcos. Among those who managed to steer a middle course between the two factions were the Rotariis or Roeros, the Asinaris, the Nattas, the Pellettas and the Luciis.

We will come across some of them again if we return to Alba not along the heavily trafficked and built-up A33-SS231, but instead the road (or the footpath along the river) that passes through the villages along the Tanaro's left bank. Here we pass through the lands that for centuries were ruled by multiple branches of the "Lombard" Roeros, whose name was used for a number of towns – Monteu Roero, Montaldo Roero, Santo Stefano Roero – while others (Magliano Alfieri, San Martino Alfieri) preserve the memory of the rule of Alfieri di Sostegno family. We recommend a brief detour to the upper part of Magliano, which offers a splendid view and a beautiful castle (publicly owned, restored and open to visitors). The castle is home to an unusual museum of plaster ceilings, displaying extraordinary examples of rural craftsmanship recovered during decades of research on both banks of the Tanaro by volunteers from Magliano Alfieri's Gruppo Spontaneo.

Alba-Vezza d'Alba-Canale-Montà-Alba

The Rocks, Arneis and the Truffle Museum

☞ This itinerary takes place entirely along the left bank of the Tanaro. The name "Roero" for this subdistrict only took root about 40 years ago; before the common term was Oltretanaro ("other side of the Tanaro"), in relation to Alba, on the river's right bank. Local scholars, meanwhile, still use Astisio, Astigiana or Terre di Chiesa, in other words historically subject to the diocese of Asti. Roero is therefore a recent name, which does not relate to geographical features (morphologically the area belongs to the Monferrato) nor historical heritage: it is simply the name of the powerful family of counts, perhaps of Germanic origin, subdivided into various branches, who for centuries ruled over these lands.

A ridge of magnificent gorges, known as *le Rocche*, the rocks, carved out by erosion dating back to the Tertiary era, cuts through the Roero from Bra to Cisterna d'Asti. The area's first hiking path runs along the rocks, opened years ago thanks to the efforts of environmentalist committee Verderoero. Many others have since been added, run by municipalities, tourism boards and, especially, the Eco-Museum of the Rocks, based in Montà. Where the land is cultivated, it mostly produces grapes for wine, other fruit (peaches, strawberries) and vegetables. Nebbiolo, arneis and favorita grapes are used to make respectively the red Roero DOCG and the whites Roero Arneis DOCG and Langhe Favorita DOC. Another wine, without a pedigree but nonetheless very enjoyable at the end of the meal, with cheese, desserts or ice cream, is made from a particular subvariety of brachetto and charmingly known as Birbèt, meaning lively, crafty, cheeky.

From Alba, take the 19th-century bridge over the Tanaro close to Piazza Medford (location of Alba's congress and exhibition centre) and at the first roundabout head towards Canale, along the former SS29 which links Turin to Cortemilia and Savona. The road is too busy to be safe for cyclists, who must do what they can to seek out alternatives, either heading towards Monticello, Piobesi and Corneliano d'Alba, or Guarene, Castagnito and Castellinaldo. We recommend these quieter routes for a return by car as well.

Our intermediate stop is the educational truffle wood in Valtesio, near Vezza d'Alba. A walk of an hour and three quarters along the *sentiero del trifolao*, the "truffle-hunter's path", leads there from Piazza San Martino, in the old part of the village, in front of the town hall and the Roero nature museum. From Borbore, the lower hamlet of Vezza, next to the former main road, the "Madernassa pear path" instead leads to the place where, in 1784, a lucky graft created the pear variety typical to the area.

Apart from grapes, however, the fruit with the greatest importance in the Roero's economy is the peach. Peach growing and the peach market are – or used to be – focused around Canale, the only town in this area with more than 5,000 inhabitants. Peach cultivation developed in Roero from the start of the 20th century, as a reaction to a hailstorm that devastated the few vines that had escaped the ravages of phylloxera. For around 70 years Canale was one of Italy's peach capitals, with a busy daily market dedicated to the fruit. Eventually however, grapes again prevailed, particularly after the classification of the denominations of origins and the surprising success of Arneis, one of Piedmont's few dry white wines.

The layout of the 13th-century expansion, the *villanova*, can still be made out in Canale's well-kept historic centre. The main axis is Via Roma, a porticoed street lined with laudably preserved houses and shops with original fixtures and fittings. The castle, formerly of the Roeros, still belongs to the descendants of the Malabaila counts, the Canalese branch of the powerful family from Asti. A former nursery school has been turned into the Roero Regional Enoteca, home to a Michelin-starred restaurant and an osteria serving traditional cuisine. The enoteca is a driving force behind promotional activities aimed not just at marketing the area's grapes and wines, but also the whole area in general.

A few kilometres from Canale, Montà is the northernmost municipality in the Roero, and in the province of Cuneo. As the name suggests, the village is reached by a steep climb. These days it is less laborious than in the past, when the village was known as *Montata fangi*, "muddy ascent". On top of the hill rises the castle of the Morras of Lavriano, established by the Roeros in the 13th century and rebuilt in Renaissance style by their successors, the Isnardis, and surrounded by a lush green park. Anyone seeking calm and a place for contemplation will find it along the road to Santo Stefano at the sanctuary of the Piloni. From here paths lead through chestnut woods to follow the chapels representing the Stations of the Cross, decorated by life-size statues. A literary prize is awarded in Montà every year, named after Carlo Cocito, a poet, journalist and local history researcher. Soon, a multimedia truffle museum will supplement the efforts of local institutions, who have already been taking advantage of the effective coordination and powerful impetus offered by the Roero Eco-museum of the Rocks.

Alba-Roddi-Verduno-Pollenzo-Cherasco La Morra-Barolo-Monforte d'Alba Monchiero-Alba

From a Sovereign's Romantic Dream to the King of Wines

This itinerary can become a loop covering the most extensive of the UNESCO-protected wine-producing sub-areas (over 30 square kilometres), taking in some of the main production hubs for the Barolo DOCG, as well as some places, geographically outside the Langhe, of great historical interest. To reach them, cross the Tanaro taking the Pollenzo bridge, parallel to the 19th-century bridge, destroyed during the last war, whose restoration has long been hoped for. By bike, it is advisable to use the cycle path that runs along the course of the river from Asti all the way to Pollenzo, while by car from Alba you will have to join the provincial road for Barolo, but at Roddi turn off onto the SP7, in the direction of Bra. Ascending to Roddi, you can enjoy beautiful views, visit the Truffle Dog University and admire the impressive castle. Once fully restored, it will host the Alba White Truffle Cooking School. Another short detour from the provincial road to Bra, turning left immediately before the little bridge over the Molino canal, leads us to Rivalta, a hamlet of La Morra, and to Verduno, a well-preserved, tranquil little village offering splendid views over the vine-covered hills. The best lookout point is the Belvedere park, at the top of the village, close to the 18th-century castle which belonged to the Savoys from 1838 to the end of the century and today houses a charming hotel and restaurant and the cellars of a winery.

Turning back to our route, we reach the municipal boundary of Bra and cross the Tanaro, leaving the Langhe behind us. Immediately after the curve on the other side of the bridge, the road continues in a straight line. Here cyclists are forced to share with cars, and can only trust in fate and the vigilant presence of speed cameras. To the left, the road is flanked by the wall of the former royal estate of Pollenzo. The privately owned castle inside the park, not open to the public, is one of the Savoy residences declared a World Heritage site by UNESCO in 1997. The ancient village of Pollenzo is an obligatory stop on our itinerary. Now administratively dependent on Bra, it was once *Pollentia*, an important Roman city dating from the 2nd century BC. In 402 AD it was the site of a battle that marked the short-lived victory of Flavius Stilicho's imperial troops over Alaric's Goths. In the Middle Ages, it fell into decline, becoming little more than a rural village, its star rising again from 1832, when Carlo Alberto of Savoy acquired the Romagnano family's possessions as part of his personal property. He undertook the ambitious task of transforming and renovating the settlement and the surrounding land, rebuilding the castle and surrounding it with other monumental buildings inspired by the medieval-revival style in fashion at the time. The large Agenzia building, formerly the central headquarters for the farm created by the king, and one of the attached farmhouses, now house the University of Gastronomic Sciences, a four-star hotel, a restaurant and – in the king's splendid cellars – the Wine Bank, a showcase of the best of Italian wines, visitable by appointment. From the main square (the Roman city's forum), faced by the Agenzia, the entrance to the castle's park and the church of San Vittore, a short walk leads to the Coliseum. In a rare, perhaps unique example of the "spontaneous recycling" of an ancient monument, over the centuries the village's modest houses have been built on top of the cavea (the underground cells) of the amphitheatre, which could hold 17,000 spectators. However, the pipes that diverted the waters of the Stura di Demonte to *Pollentia* were designed to meet the needs of a million people.

Cherasco, our next stop, is one of Piedmont's most interesting minor centres. Built from 1243 by the imperial representative Manfredi Lancia II and the podestà (governing magistrate) of Alba, Sarlo di Drua, it is laid out as a perfect square, divided into equally regular blocks, with only the imposing bulk of the Viscontis' castle breaking the order of the plan. "Among the starry walls", to borrow the title of a novel by Gina Lagorio, porticoed streets, stately palazzos and art-filled churches characterize the "city of peace treaties", ennobled by the favour shown to it over the centuries by the Savoys. They even

temporarily transferred their court here, and, in moments of danger, the Holy Shroud of Turin.
From Cherasco, which surprisingly falls within the boundaries of the Barolo DOCG zone, the valley-floor road takes you quickly to Monchiero, but we recommend you go instead via the heart of the homeland of the "king of wines and wine of kings". Having descended towards Moglia, at the first junction, instead of turning right, take the small bridge over the Tanaro – which here receives the waters of the Stura – and climb the panoramic, winding road to La Morra. The village, famous in the first decades of the last century for the "grape cure" and today for the 27 nebbiolo crus that supply its renowned wineries, probably sets a national record for the number of beds available for tourists compared to the number of residents. As you look out from the viewpoint of the highest square, it's easy to see why so many tourists want to stay here: the sweeping panorama over the hilly sea of vineyards, set against the background of the Alps, has no equal in the Bassa Langa, the lower-lying part of the Langhe.
Various footpaths and cycle routes leave from La Morra and wind through the Barolo vineyards. Near the Fontanazza village, between the Brunate and Cerequio crus, it's hard to miss the gaudy colours of the Madonna delle Grazie chapel, a centuries-old rural building, repainted in pop style by two contemporary artists, Solomon LeWitt from America and David Tremlett from Britain. Another unusual landmark,

this time natural, easily spotted from various points along the walks, is the immense cedar of Lebanon which for over 150 years has dominated the Cordero di Montezemolo family's Monfalletto estate.

Most of the "gentle" routes suggested by the Strada dei Grandi Vini di Langa association have Barolo as their terminus. The village that gave its name to the king of wines has a less panoramic location than others within the DOCG zone: perhaps the houses and castle were built within a basin so as to save the best-exposed sites for vineyards. The village is dominated by its imposing castle, formerly belonging to the Falletti marquesses, a powerful feudal dynasty that in the 19th century made a significant contribution, with Camillo Cavour, to developing

the cultivation of nebbiolo in the Langhe. As well as housing the library curated by Silvio Pellico, the castle is also home to the multimedia Wine Museum and the Barolo Regional Enoteca.
A walk of around 6 kilometres, on a mix of paved and unpaved roads, leads from Barolo to Monforte d'Alba, a pretty town whose steep medieval centre is characterized by picturesque cobbled lanes. Walking up to the top brings you to the monumental complex formed by the Palazzo Scarampi, the bell tower, a church and an oratory. The piazza's amphitheatre-like shape makes it an ideal open-air venue for summer concerts and shows.
Monforte has a connection to one of European history's most tragic stories: the persecution of the Cathars, "the pure ones", members of a religious sect declared heretical by the Roman Church. From the 11th century, they were suppressed with a determination that let to episodes of unprecedented violence. The inhabitants of Monforte, including the feudal countess Berta, were suspected of Catharism because they doubted the dogma of the Trinity and denied the need for sacraments and therefore the clergy. And so in 1028, soldiers acting on Archbishop Ariberto d'Intimiano's orders seized the castle, set it on fire and deported the entire population to Milan. The many who refused to forsake their beliefs were burned at the stake in front of one of Milan's city gates, ever since known as Porta Monforte, connected to Piazza San Babila by Corso Monforte.
Descending towards the Tanaro's valley floor, do not forget to make a quick visit to Monchiero Alto, a tiny, peaceful and well-preserved village, for centuries the retreat of painter Eso Peluzzi (Cairo Montenotte 1894-Monchiero 1985).
The return to Alba offers various possibilities: for a triumphal conclusion to your tour of the Barolo hills, we recommend heading for Grinzane Cavour, where the young Camillo Benso was mayor for 17 years, using the extensive family land (almost 500 acres) to put to good use his skills as a far-sighted agricultural entrepreneur, winegrower and wine merchant. The beautiful rectangular castle, specifically recognized by UNESCO as a World Heritage site, houses the Piedmontese Regional Enoteca and, every November, hosts the International Alba White Truffle Auction.

Alba-Bossolasco-Murazzano-Dogliani-Alba

The Land of Dolcetto and Sheep's Toma

☞ Dolcetto boasts a record eight possible denominations, twice as many if we take into account the additional classifications (Superiore, Vigna). The wine is made from the red grape of the same name in the provinces of Cuneo (Dolcetto d'Alba, di Diano d'Alba, di Dogliani, Pinerolese), Asti (d'Asti, d'Alba), Alessandria (d'Acqui, di Ovada) and Turin (Pinerolese). A classic wine for the whole meal, not too challenging, along with Barbera it is a favourite of Piedmont's older generations. Outside the region, its potential sales have perhaps been harmed by its name, which suggests a sweet (*dolce*) wine, while in fact it can even have a slight and very pleasant bitterness. The origin of the name, the dialect terms *dosset* and *dozzet*, refer in fact to the high sugar content of the grape, mentioned for the first time in a municipal decree from 1593 and later in 1799 in the *Istruzioni sulla coltivazione della vite e sulla migliore conservazione dei vini* ("Instructions for cultivating vines and the best preservation of wines") by Giuseppe Nuvolone-Pergamo, director of the Experimental Garden of the Royal Agriculture Society of Turin.

This itinerary is dedicated to this traditional variety and its enjoyable wines. It leads from the lower Bassa Langa of vineyards and cattle to the upper Alta Langa of hazelnuts and sheep's milk cheeses, and is designed as a loop. By taking the SP32 and returning with the former SS661 and the SP3 (by car or motorcycle; unfortunately the less-busy routes for bicycles are fragmentary and inconvenient) you can also include Dogliani, a vibrant little town on the border between the Albese and Monregalese areas, and capital of one of the Dolcetto varieties. To first visit the home of Dolcetto di Diano d'Alba, when leaving Alba and taking the

former SS29 (not SP429), do not head immediately for the hamlet of Ricca, but instead go slightly west to reach Diano. The village is less than 500 metres above sea level, but a rise near the main piazza offers ample views over the Barolo, Barbaresco and Moscato hills and an extensive section of the Alpine arc.
Passing via Rodello or Montelupo Albese, also with good views, we reach Tre Cunei. Here the road, running almost straight, takes us along a kind of plateau (unfortunately flanked by incongruous conglomerations of buildings) to another beautiful little village, Serravalle Langhe, and to Bossolasco. Considered the most important centre in this part of the Alta Langa (overall the area's main reference point is Cortemilia, in the Bormida Valley), this municipality of 700 inhabitants is known by two nicknames, the pearl of the Langhe and the village of roses. The second name becomes immediately clear when you see the dozens of plants climbing up the stone walls of the mostly 18th-century houses along Via Umberto, to very picturesque effect. As for "the pearl of the Langhe", Bossolasco earned that label by attracting a great number of illustrious guests, who came for the freshness provided by its altitude (750 metres above sea level), the beauty of its landscape, its carefully preserved buildings and – not least – its early attention to quality food and wine tourism. Visitors have included Luigi Einaudi, Giuseppe Saragat, Giuseppe Ungaretti, Italo Calvino, Mario Soldati, Renato Guttuso and the group of painters (Francesco Menzio, Carlo Levi, Gigi Chessa, Enrico Paulucci, Guido Botta, Irene Invrea) who decades ago chose the village as their preferred residence. The writer Beppe Fenoglio stayed here in autumn 1962, hoping in vain for an improvement in his lung disease. Used to the rural isolation of his visits to San Benedetto Belbo, and the harsh peasant life in the Langhe reflected in his novels, however, he considered the village of the roses "too worldly". This judgement will not surprise anyone who is familiar with the aspiration of the author of *Johnny the Partisan* to be "a soldier of Cromwell, with a Bible in my pack and a gun over my shoulder", and which speaks volumes about the austere

and intransigent component, even a little Calvinist, of the Piedmontese character.

Fenoglio also has connections with our itinerary's next stop, where he spent some childhood summers and the first part of his partisan service. This is Murazzano, at the same altitude as Bossolasco and with only a few more inhabitants, a similarly beautiful landscape and a well-preserved medieval tower. The village gives its name to one of the province's most celebrated PDO cheeses, Murazzano, traditionally made with sheep's milk. The PDO regulations, however, allow the addition of up to 40% cow's milk. A Slow Food Presidium has revived the historic version of the cheese, using the name "Langhe sheep tuma" to refer to the cheese made with raw milk from the Langhe sheep breed. Once very common, the breed's numbers have now been reduced to barely 2,000 animals between Piedmont and Liguria. The sheep's milk can be supplemented by no more than 5% goat's milk. The tuma is made in the spring and summer; a cylindrical cheese, weighing between 200 to 300 grams, it has no rind and a soft, straw-white paste. Tumas are consumed after 10 or 15 days of aging, but they can also be stored in glass jars (*burnìe*). Alternatively, if the cheeses are aged for at least a month, they can be broken up or grated, mixed with a little grappa and packed into earthenware containers to make *bross*, a piquant fermented spread.

Before returning to Alba via Monchiero, Barolo and Gallo Grinzane, it's worth spending a few hours visiting Dogliani, a town of around 5,000 inhabitants on the banks of the River Rea. The medieval core, still recognizable in the entrance gates to the Borgo, the lower part of the old town (the highest part of the settlement is called Castello), has, as everywhere, been built over by successive layers of architecture from different eras. Here, however, the magnificent works of Giovanni Battista Schellino, a brilliant exponent of 19th-century eclecticism, provide a distinctive and very original touch. Not far from the main square, along the Rea, the Luigi Einaudi library, donated in 1963 to the municipality by the statesman's family, is used as an innovative tool for civic assimilation and is still an important hub for meetings and debates.

Alba-Ceva-Priero-Montezemolo-Mombarcaro Niella Belbo-Feisoglio-Cravanzana-Alba

A View of the Sea (Perhaps) from the Roof of the Langhe

*

☞ This itinerary shares the first stretch, to Passo della Bossola, with the previous route. Afterwards however, instead of turning right towards Murazzano, we continue to the Colle della Pedaggera and descend through lovely landscapes to Ceva.

Located at the point where the Cevetta joins the Tanaro, amidst the southern spurs of the Langhe and the Mondovì hills, this small town (population circa 5,800) has an illustrious past. The old medieval centre, with low porticoes, pointed arches, loggias and vaults, provides ample evidence. Already a Roman *municipium*, from the 12th century Ceva was the capital of a marquessate formed following the division of the possessions of Bonifacio del Vasto, one of the descendants of Aleramo, the legendary founder of the family whose various branches ruled the Monferrato, Saluzzo, Savona and other lands between Piedmont and Liguria. Located a few kilometres from the border with Liguria, Ceva's natural role as a link with the sea was accentuated by rail lines opened in the years following Unification, and confirmed in the 1960s by the construction of the Turin-Savona A6 motorway. Though primarily a place for passing through, it still attracts people from the surrounding towns and villages, and is known for its mushroom trade. The woods of the Alta Langa, the upper Valtanaro and the Mongia and Cevetta valleys are full of the fungi. Since 1961, a large mushroom fair has been held every year on the third Sunday of September, organized by the local mycology group. This event has helped Ceva earn the nickname of "the mushroom capital". An important white truffle market is also held here, and nearby Mondovì dedicates a regional fair to the prized underground fungus, paired every two years with the gastronomic festival Peccati di Gola (literally "sins of gluttony").

Following the course of the Cevetta, along the SP430, a slip road connecting the important Colle di Nava and Colle di Cadibona roads, or by footpath, we reach the truffle woodland in Priero restored by the Study Centre. This small village, with a population of a little over 500, deserves to be better known, given its pretty medieval centre, with a regular chessboard layout, porticoed central street and large tower. Its circumference the same as its height, the tower is a remnant of the castle that once rose from the walls.

At our next destination, Montezemolo, close to the border with the province of Savona, we first reach the village of Tetti, the location of the town hall; the other built-up area, Villa, is the site of the 18th-century home of the Cordero marquesses. The Belbo, is just a few kilometres from here, in a wet, wooded area, a protected natural reserve with interesting flora and fauna. Hiking, horse-riding, mountain biking and, in the winter, cross-country skiing are all possible here.

Montezemolo is famous for its honey. Along with other bee products and beekeeping equipment, honey is the focus of a regional fair held every year in early July. Climbing to the 896-metre-altitude of Mombarcaro, the "roof of the Langhe", meanwhile, we find the Upper Belbo Valley potato, promoted by a consortium which organizes a fair in mid-July with the local tourism association to pay tribute to the flavourful mountain tuber. The village, founded in the Middle Ages, is worth a visit for the extraordinary panoramic views it offers. The Mombarcaro hill, the highest point in the Langhe, rises isolated between the Belbo and Bormida slopes, dominating its surroundings. From up here, the gaze can range from the peaks of the Alps to the hilly spurs with their thousand chromatic nuances, coming one after the other like the sea's waves. On the clearest, sunniest day, particularly when the *marin* wind blows from Liguria, you can even make out the glimmering of the real sea, beyond Savona, distant but instantly recognizable.

The route to return to Alba passes through other pretty villages – Niella Belbo, Feisoglio, Cravanzana – but the most lasting memory of our tour will be that water sparkling in the sun. In any other part of the world, it would be a mirage, but here, in the magical land of the Langhe, it is real.

Recipes

  TRADITIONAL  CREATIVE

Tajarin all'albese
Alba Tajarin Pasta

Serves 4

500 g Italian type 0 or plain flour, 3 whole eggs and 5 egg yolks, salt, extra-virgin olive oil, 2 handfuls of cornmeal, butter at room temperature, 40 g Alba white truffle

1 hour, plus resting time for the pasta

Mound the flour in a heap on a wooden pastry board, then make a hollow in the middle. Beat together the eggs and yolks with a little salt. Pour the mixture into the flour hollow. Drizzle over some extra-virgin olive oil, then, using a fork at first, mix the ingredients together well. Wet the hands in warm water (extra water should not be added to the dough) and knead the dough carefully and at length, until it becomes smooth and homogenous. Divide the dough into fist-sized balls. Leave them to rest, covered with a cloth, for a couple of hours.
Use a rolling pin or pasta machine to roll the pasta balls into very thin sheets. Leave to rest for a few minutes, then sprinkle with a little cornmeal (reserving one handful) and roll them up. Using a large, sharp knife, cut each roll into very thin slices, then unroll the noodles onto a wooden board, sprinkling them with the remaining cornmeal.
Bring a large pan of water to the boil. Meanwhile melt the butter over a very low heat. When the water is boiling, salt it and add the pasta. Drain after no more than two or three minutes, transfer to a tureen and toss with the melted butter.
Divide the pasta between pre-heated soup plates. Use a truffle slicer to shave an equal amount of Alba white truffle over each portion.

Along with agnolotti, tajarin *(Piedmontese tagliolini) are the Langhe's most famous fresh pasta. They are made from white flour and plenty of eggs. The proportions we suggest are standard, but some recipes double them, while the truly legendary* tajarin *require 40 yolks for every kilo of flour, making the dough very hard to handle. Long and very thin – sometimes even thinner than the one-millimetre thickness of* capelli d'angelo *(angel's hair) – as this recipe recommends, they should be cut by hand, after rolling up the sheet of dough. This operation requires precision, skill and an experience that is sadly increasingly hard to find. In the Langhe and the Monferrato, the classic sauces are butter and sage, a roast meat gravy or chicken livers. But of course white truffle is the most precious of seasonings.*

Uova al Burro
Eggs Fried in Butter

Serves 4

8 eggs, 100 g butter, salt,
40 g Alba white truffle

10 minutes

The eggs must be very fresh. If kept in the refrigerator, take them out at least an hour in advance and let them come to room temperature. Melt the butter in a frying pan over low heat. When it starts to foam, but before it changes colour, break the eggs into the pan. Salt the eggs, and continue cooking over medium heat for five or six minutes, every so often carefully cutting into the egg white with a wooden spatula so that it cooks evenly.
Use a slotted spoon to remove the eggs from the pan and arrange them on individual plates. Scatter over a showering of truffle shavings and serve immediately.

There are two other ways to prepare eggs as a base for Alba white truffles. The first is to poach them. In a wide, shallow metal saucepan, heat salted water, acidulated with a little white-wine vinegar. When it begins to boil, crack in the eggs and lower the heat, bringing the water temperature to 95°C. After three or four minutes, drain them with a slotted spoon, arrange them on plates and tidy up any frayed whites. Before sprinkling them with truffle shavings, they can be topped with brown butter. Using special silicon egg-poaching moulds will give a neater and more elegant appearance, as they prevent the white from spreading into the water and produce a more compact egg.
The second way is to cook them en cocotte. *For every egg, you will need a small round oven-proof ramekin. Heat the ramekins and grease them with a piece of butter. Break one egg inside each ramekin and add a pinch of salt and a grinding of pepper, them top with a small piece of butter and place in a high-sided roasting tin. Fill to half the height of the ramekins with boiling water, then cover with aluminium foil and bake at 220°C, or on top of the stove, for around six minutes. If you get the cooking time right, and keep the water just barely at a boil, the white should set softly and the yolk should remain runny. Once again, before topping with truffles they can be drizzled with brown butter.*

Fonduta
Italian Fondue

Serves 4

400 g Valle d'Aosta Fontina (not too aged),
750 ml milk, 50 g butter, 4 egg yolks, pepper,
60 g Alba white truffle, toasted bread

30 minutes, plus steeping time for the cheese

Cut the Fontina into cubes or very thin slices. Place in a container and cover with milk. Keep somewhere cool for five or six hours, or overnight.
Place the butter, egg yolks and cheese in a shallow saucepan, with a ladleful of the milk from the cheese and a pinch of pepper. Place the saucepan in a larger pan of boiling water. Over low heat, beat the mixture vigorously with a wooden spoon or a whisk. The cheese will melt, forming strings, then thicken. Just as it thickens into a smooth cream, remove from the heat. Serve immediately, topped with truffle shavings, with toasted bread.

"Take 4 hectograms of the full-fat cheese known as Fontina, with the rind cut off, [...] melt the Fontina slowly over a low flame, stirring until melted and smooth, [...] stir hard over the flame until the strings forming the Fontina are broken and it becomes liquid, and it will soon become thick and smooth like a cream, but never let it boil, [...] serve it with 60 grams of good white truffles, cleaned and cut into thin slices, half mixed with the Fontina and half scattered on top." So writes Giovanni Vialardi, chef to Carlo Alberto and Vittorio Emanuele II, in Trattato di cucina pasticcera *(Turin 1854), describing the dish that makes the simplest and most refined use of the Valle d'Aosta's most typical cheese. But fonduta is not so much a legacy of the food culture of the mountainous region just north of Turin. Rather, it is a borrowing from the cuisine that established itself in the Savoy dominions at the foot of the mountains by adapting rustic and bourgeois models from France (Valais fondue, raclette). The pairing between the flavourful cheese and the most prized of truffles produces a dish that is not only rich and fortifying, but which can also be served as an antipasto, a main course or as a one-dish meal, in varying quantities.*

Insalata di Carne Cruda
Piedmontese Veal Tartare

Serves 4

400 g Piedmontese-breed (Fassone) veal rump,
1 garlic clove, extra-virgin olive oil,
salt and pepper, 40 g Alba white truffle

10 minutes, plus chopping time for the meat

The cut of veal must be very lean, and should not be ground in a meat grinder, but chopped very finely using a large knife until minced. Squash the garlic clove and use it to rub the bottom and sides of a salad bowl (grilèt), then add the meat, seasoning it with extra-virgin olive oil (which can be of any provenance, but must have a delicate flavour), salt and a little pepper. Mix together well, ideally by hand, then transfer the meat to a serving dish and cover it with thin slices of white truffle. Serve immediately.

The irreplaceable star of this dish is veal from Piedmontese cattle. This breed is mostly farmed in the southern part of the region (provinces of Cuneo, Asti and parts of Turin and Alessandria). The most interesting part of its story begins in 1886, when a spontaneous mutation caused a bull with enormous haunches to be born on a farm in Guarene, a few kilometres from Alba. This muscle growth characteristic is known as "horse rump" or "double rump". The bull was the origin of the vitello della coscia *(literally "veal of the thigh") or Fassone breed. The latter name comes from the French façon, the technical term for cattle characterized by overdeveloped muscular masses. The Piedmontese thus evolved from a triple-purpose breed (meat, milk and draught) to a beef breed, prized for its excellent yield. The meat is high in iron and antioxidants and low in fat with minimal connective tissue, making it extraordinarily tender. A Slow Food Presidium was set up to protect and promote the breed in 1998. Run by the La Granda association, based in Fossano, near Cuneo, it unites farmers who have committed to raising their animals following a strict production protocol, adopting a cow-calf system (closed cycle) and using only natural feed (hay and cereals, with no silage or industrial feed).* Insalata di carne cruda, *literally "raw meat salad", is a minimalist dish. In the Langhe, it used to only be served generously to women who had just given birth and convalescents. It was Giacomo Morra who included the dish among the Savona's antipasti, opening the way for the recipe's success. Indeed, it is now found all over Italy, both with and without truffles.*

Risotto Bianco alla Piemontese
Piedmontese White Risotto

Serves 4

half an onion, 1 l beef broth, 100 g butter,
320 g short-grain rice (Arborio, Baldo, Carnaroli or Roma),
1/2 glass of dry white wine, salt, 40 g Alba white truffle

30 minutes

Peel and finely mince the onion. Bring the broth to a boil.
In a wide, shallow saucepan, preferably made of heavy copper or aluminium and with a long handle, heat half the butter. When it has melted, add the onion and sauté until transparent, but without letting it change colour. At this point add the rice and stir with a wooden spatula, toasting it for four or five minutes, until the grains are barely opaque. Add the wine and cook for a few minutes to evaporate the alcohol, then, over medium heat, start to add the boiling broth, one ladleful at a time. Adjust the salt, and taste frequently to check the cooking stage. The pan should be removed from the heat when the last point of resistance of the rice grain's inner core of starch is just about to soften, but still maintains some elasticity. Off the heat, stir in the remaining butter. Distribute the risotto between heated soup bowls, then bring to the table with the truffle and the truffle slicer, allowing every diner to serve themselves – hopefully with moderation – as they please.

Piedmont is Italy's top rice-growing region, and Italy the biggest rice producer in Europe. This cereal grain of Asian origin is now grown on a large scale on every continent and represents the main food resource for the people of Southeast Asia. It has found an ideal habitat in the section of the Po Valley bounded by Dora Baltea and Ticino. The first province to grow rice, however, was not Vercelli or Novara in Piedmont, now famous for the grain, but Pavia in Lombardy. In recent years, rice has also begun to be grown on a small scale in the far northwest of the Alba-Bra area (within the municipalities of Bra and Sanfrè). Independently of the proximity of the paddies, rice – particularly in the exclusively Italian form of risotto – has a significant place in Piedmontese cooking, particularly in bourgeois recipes. Topping risotto with white truffles is the ultimate culmination for a dish that conveys a sense of refined opulence despite its simple ingredients and straightforward execution.

Salt Cod Fillet with Porcini, Caesar's Mushrooms and Alba White Truffle

Ugo Alciati, Ristorante Guido, Villa Reale di Fontanafredda
Serralunga d'Alba

Serves 4

200 g potatoes, 100 g fresh porcini mushrooms,
100 g Caesar's mushrooms, extra-virgin olive oil, salt and pepper,
300 g desalted salt cod, 10 parsley leaves, 1 Alba white truffle

50 minutes

Wash the potatoes and boil them in salted water until tender. Clean the porcini and Caesar's mushrooms, cut them into thin slices and sauté them in a frying pan with a little olive oil. Season with salt and pepper, then continue cooking, covered, for six or seven minutes over high heat. Cut the salt cod into four pieces and steam for five minutes with the skin side down. Puree the parsley with a little olive oil. Drain the potatoes, peel them, pass them through a potato ricer and divide them between four serving plates. Lay the salt cod on top and surround with the mushrooms. Sprinkle over a few drops of parsley oil. Top with thin shavings of white truffle.

Three types of fungi accompany salt cod, known as baccalà *in Italy, in this recipe from the restaurant named after the great Guido Alciati. Originally housed in the royal complex built by Carlo Alberto in Pollenzo, the restaurant has now moved to another prestigious historic building, the Villa Reale on the Fontanafredda estate. In line with its characteristics and the gastronomic tradition, the white truffle is used raw, to refine the dish, while the mushrooms are briefly cooked. They belong to the two most-prized species of wild mushrooms:* Boletus edulis *(porcini, known as* bolé *in Piedmontese) and* Amanita caesarea, *Caesar's mushroom (in Italian* ovolo, ovolo buono *or* fungo reale *and in Piedmontese* cocón *or* bolé real*). The latter has an exquisite taste, but is also one of the fungi most sensitive to environmental degradation. As a result, it is disappearing from the woods and from home and restaurant kitchens.*

Gavi di Gavi

Slow-Cooked Eggs with Parmesan Foam, Langhe Hazelnuts and Alba White Truffle

Alessandro Boglione, Ristorante Al Castello
Grinzane Cavour

Serves 4

4 egg yolks, 250 g milk, 250 g single cream, 3 whole eggs, 100 g grated Parmigiano-Reggiano, 20 g toasted and chopped Tonda Gentile delle Langhe hazelnuts, 20 g Alba white truffle

40 minutes

Place the egg yolks in a baking dish full of water and cook in a steam oven at a temperature of 65°C for 25 minutes.
Meanwhile, mix together the milk, cream, whole eggs and grated Parmigiano. Cook in a bain-marie for three or four minutes at 72°C, leave to cool and then strain. Pour the mixture in a siphon and charge it with two cartridges.
Drain the cooked yolks and lay each one in the bottom of a cocktail glass. Using the siphon, fill the glass with foam. Top with hazelnuts and truffle shavings.

We described the traditional way in the note on p.138, and now here is the most modern method for poaching eggs (though only the yolks are used in this recipe). Slow cooking at a low temperature is a technique spreading to non-professional kitchens, because it allows food to be cooked gently, without assaulting it, maintaining its softness and original colour while intensifying the flavour. This recipe uses both a technologically advanced cooking method – steam oven – and a system, the bain-marie or double boiler, that can be set up on the stovetop and was already common in home cooking in our grandmothers' time.
The simple dish presented by Alessandro Boglione, the Bra-born chef of the restaurant in the Grinzane castle, a UNESCO World Heritage site, uses no "exotic" ingredients. Eggs, milk and other dairy products (cream and Parmigiano Reggiano, the most celebrated of Italian grating cheeses, mentioned in cookbooks and literary texts since the 14th century) are joined by two products very typical of the local area: Alba white truffle and Tonda Gentile delle Langhe hazelnuts. A protected geographical indication (Piemonte) recognizes the

excellence of these nuts, whose production is concentrated around the upper valleys of the Tanaro, the Bormida and the Belbo. The variety, considered one of the world's best, has a medium-thick shell, fairly pale in colour and opaque, with many streaks. The nut is round and easily peeled, and once toasted has a subtle but lingering flavour. An irreplaceable ingredient in the region's renowned confectionery, it is an essential element in gelato, creams and gianduia chocolate.

100% Viognier

Potato Puree with Lapsang Souchong Tea, Quail's Eggs and Alba White Truffle

Enrico Crippa, Ristorante Piazza Duomo
Alba

Serves 4

10 g Lapsang Souchong (smoked Chinese black tea), 4 quail's eggs, 150 g yellow-fleshed potatoes, sea salt, 100 g mountain (or single) cream, muscovado sugar, Alba white truffle

2 hours, plus egg marinating time

Finely mince the tea leaves. Bring 500 ml of water to 95°C. Add 5 grams of tea and leave to infuse for five minutes. Strain and cool. Boil the quail's eggs in 65°C water for 12 minutes. Remove immediately from the pan and immerse them in ice water. Using a sharp knife and a teaspoon, peel them and leave them to marinate in the cold tea for 12 hours. Wash the potatoes and boil them in salted water until tender. Drain, peel and place in a Thermomix. Bring to 90°C, add the cream and salt to taste. Place a pinch of sugar in the bottom of four small glasses. Carefully place a tea-marinated quail's egg in each glass. Cover with the hot potato puree and finish with a sprinkling of the remaining tea and a generous grating of white truffle.

Enrico Crippa's biccherino *(little glass) uses both local and exotic ingredients. Potatoes are a New World food, adopted after many centuries of delay in continental Europe. They became popular in France thanks to the efforts of pharmacist Antoine-Augustin Parmentier and in Italy of Antonio Zanon from Friuli and Vincenzo Virginio from Cuneo. The quail's eggs could in theory represent additional spoils from a hunting trip, but by now* Coturnix coturnix *has become more farmed poultry than wild game bird, so the eggs are found fairly easily in shops. The globalization of the markets also makes it relatively easy to procure Lapsang Souchong tea and muscovado sugar, even though one comes from China's Wuyi mountains and the other from the Philippines. Crippa suggests a wine made from 100% riesling renano (the Italian name for white riesling).*

Riesling Renano

Liquid Cardoon and Anchovy Tortelli with Alba White Truffle

Maurilio Garola, Ristorante La Ciau del Tornavento
Treiso

Serves 6

Filling: 3 ribs of Nizza Monferrato hunchbacked cardoon, milk, salt and pepper, 2 salted anchovies, extra-virgin olive oil, 30 g melted Alpine butter, 50 g sheep's milk ricotta
Pasta: 250 g Italian 00-type or other superfine flour, 120 g durum wheat semolina, 12 egg yolks, 10 g fine salt, 1 tbsp extra-virgin olive oil
Garnish: melted butter, Alba white truffle

1 hour, plus pasta resting time

Clean the cardoons, removing as many of the tough fibres as possible. Cut into pieces and cook for 50 minutes in a mixture of salted water and milk. Desalt the anchovies and remove the backbone. While the cardoons cook, prepare the pasta dough. Mix together the flour and semolina and mound into a pile on a wooden board. Make a hollow in the centre and add the yolks, salt and olive oil, then mix together, kneading at length to form a smooth dough. Form into a ball and leave to rest, covered, while preparing the filling. Drain the cardoons, cut them into 1-centimetre squares and brown in a deep frying pan with extra-virgin olive oil. Add the butter and anchovies and continue cooking for another five minutes. Puree the mixture in a food processor, then pass through a sieve. Once completely cooled, stir in the ricotta and season to taste with salt and pepper. Use a rolling pin or pasta machine to roll the dough into a thin sheet. Using a smooth, round pasta cutter, cut out circles around 2 centimetres in diameter. Place a knob of the filling in the middle of each one. Form them into tortelli, or, for a simpler version, fold over to make half-moons, pressing firmly around the edge to make sure they stay closed during cooking. Cook briefly in boiling salted water, drain and toss with melted butter. Serve with shavings of truffle.

Maurilio Garola's tortelli are "liquid" because the filling is much less dense than the classic version. The other innovation is the mix of wheats used in the dough (northern Italian filled pastas generally

use only regular wheat flour), while the other ingredients are traditionally Piedmontese. Cardoons are very typical of the region, grown in the sandy soil in the Belbo Valley, in and around Nizza Monferrato. A traditional technique is used to whiten the stalks, making them tender and giving them a "hunchbacked" appearance. Protected by a Slow Food Presidium, it is the only cardoon variety that can also be eaten raw, and is an essential accompaniment to the anchovy-and-garlic dip bagna caoda.

Verduno Pelaverga

Chestnut Cappuccino, Seared Scallops, Savoury Biscuits and Alba White Truffle

Masayuki Kondo, Ristorante Locanda del Pilone
Località Madonna di Como, Alba

Serves 4

Savoury biscuits: 37 g room-temperature butter, 50 g Italian 00-type flour or other superfine flour, 10 g milk, 4 g egg yolk, 8 g sugar, 1 g salt
Cappuccino: 10 g minced shallot, extra-virgin olive oil, 10 g roasted chestnuts, 30 g single cream, 300 g milk, salt
To serve: 4 scallops, salt, 80 g milk, 10 g Alba white truffle

30 minutes, plus resting time for the dough

Start by making the biscuits. Mix the softened butter with half of the flour. Add the milk, egg yolk, sugar and salt. Continuing to stir gently, add the remaining flour. Mix for another minute, then cover with cling film and refrigerate for half a day. Roll out the dough to a thickness of 3 millimetres and cut out biscuits. Lay them on a baking tray, poke them with a fork and bake in a 175°C/Gas Mark 3 oven for 12-13 minutes. Meanwhile, make the cappuccino. Sweat the shallot in a little olive oil. Add the chestnuts and sauté, then add the cream, milk and 200 ml water. When the chestnuts have softened, puree the mixture, pass through a sieve and salt to taste.
Open the scallop shells and take out the scallops. Rinse well, pat dry, cut into four pieces, salt lightly and sear in a frying pan for no more than a minute. Heat the chestnut cream. Bring the milk to 60°C and use an immersion blender to foam it. Place the scallops in a cappuccino cup. Pour over the chestnut cream and the foamy milk. In the middle, place the crumbled biscuits and top with a shaving of white truffles.

Cappuccino usually refers to an espresso coffee lengthened with hot milk that has been frothed up with pressurized steam. The colour recalls the habits of Capuchin friars, the origin of the name. Popular with Italians at breakfast, foreign tourists have also adopted it as an after-dinner drink, as an alternative to espresso.

These days, restaurants have also started to call "cappuccino" any dish, usually savoury, which has the same creamy-liquid consistency as a cappuccino and is served in a similar cup or small glass. This is the case with Masayuki Kondo's cappuccino. The Japanese chef from the Locanda del Pilone combines very different ingredients in the recipe: chestnuts, the fruit of a tree that grows in the hills and mountains, along with scallops, prized shellfish from the sea. The two are united by Alba white truffles.

Young Barbera d'Alba

Raschera Fondue with Seared Porcini and Alba White Truffles

Elide Mollo and Enrico Cordero, Ristorante Il Centro
Priocca

Serves 6

50 g grated Parmigiano Reggiano, 300 g porcini mushrooms, 1 minced garlic clove, chopped herbs (thyme, marjoram, rosemary), salt, 2 tbsps extra-virgin olive oil, 500 g mountain Raschera, 500 ml milk, 1 egg yolk, 1 Alba white truffle

1 hour

Heat a non-stick frying pan, then sprinkle in a thin layer of grated Parmigiano Reggiano in the shape of a circle around 10 centimetres in diameter. Heat for a few minutes, then just as the cheese starts to melt, delicately remove the disc with a spatula and transfer to a wire rack to cool and harden. Repeat to make a total of 6 discs. Clean the porcini mushrooms and cut them into slices about 1 centimetre thick. Toss with the garlic, herbs and salt. Heat the olive oil in a frying pan, then sear the mushrooms on both sides. Cut the Raschera into cubes and place in a heatproof bowl with the milk. Heat over a bain-marie until the cheese melts and the mixture becomes smooth. Remove from the heat, and whisk in the egg yolk. Continue whisking until emulsified. Pour the cheese mixture into shallow soup plates and lay the porcini on top. Garnish with a Parmigiano crisp and finish with white truffle shavings.

The fonduta served at Il Centro in Priocca, a Roero village near the border with the province of Asti, does not deviate far from tradition. The biggest difference is the use of Raschera instead of Fontina, by now fairly common in the region's restaurants. Perhaps it is a way to emphasize the Piedmontese identity of a dish whose original version uses a typical cheese from the mountains of Valle d'Aosta. Raschera is named after an Alpine pasture at the foot of the Mongioie, a chalky mountain that rises 2,630 metres at the watershed between the Tanaro, Ellero and Corsaglia valleys. Typical of the mountain dairies around Mondovì, it is a medium-fat cheese, made ideally with raw milk from Bruno Alpina or Piedmontese cows.

The paste is soft, elastic and ivory white in colour, with a thin rind, reddish-grey in colour, sometimes yellowish. The square or round forms can be marked as "d'alpeggio" if they are made at altitudes above 900 metres in 10 municipalities around Mondovì. In addition to Alba white truffles, husband-and-wife Enrico Cordero and Elide Mollo also pair the fonduta with porcini mushrooms, which grow abundantly – though less abundantly than in the past – in the hilly and mountainous woods in the province of Cuneo.

Dolcetto d'Alba

Buttered Root Vegetables with Black and White Truffles

Davide Palluda, Ristorante All'Enoteca
Canale

Serves 6

100 g Chinese artichokes (crosnes), 100 g Jerusalem artichokes, 100 g celeriac, 100 g beetroot, 100 g lettuce root, 100 g chicory root, 1 l milk, salt, 1 Périgord or Norcia black truffle, extra-virgin olive oil, Marsala Vergine (solera method), beef broth, butter, grated Parmigiano Reggiano, 1 Alba white truffle

1 hour

Carefully trim and wash all the roots. Cut them into large pieces. Blanch each one separately in the milk mixed with a litre of salted water. Drain when al dente. Sauté the black truffle, sliced into shavings, in a little extra-virgin olive oil. Pour over a little Marsala and let evaporate. Add a few spoonfuls of broth and continue cooking briefly, then puree until smooth. Sauté the roots in a frying pan with butter and some grated Parmigiano. Arrange them attractively on serving plates, dot with the black truffle sauce and cover with thin shavings of Alba white truffle.

Don't let the exotic names of some of the ingredients in this rich yet simple starter fool you: Jerusalem artichoke is commonly known in Italy as topinambur, *and in Piedmont is a traditional accompaniment to the anchovy-and-garlic dip* bagna caoda. *Chinese artichoke is the common name for the root of a plant native to the Far East,* Stachys affinis, *also known as* S. sieboldii, *brought to Europe in the mid 19th century, which reached the Turinese hills from France. The secret to the dish, ennobled by the prized black and white truffles, lies in the balance of flavours between the roots: the bitter chicory, the sweet lettuce and beetroot and the aromatic celeriac and pseudo-artichokes.*

Timorasso dei Colli Tortonesi